Greenwich
Terry
Lisa
Sam
Emma

Let's go 1

von Carl Taylor sowie Marion Horner
und Elizabeth Daymond

Herausgeber: Dr. Werner Kieweg, M. A.

Ernst Klett Verlag
Stuttgart Düsseldorf Leipzig

Let's go 1

Im Auftrag des Verlags herausgegeben von:
Dr. Werner Kieweg, M.A., Schwabmünchen

Erarbeitet von:
Carl Taylor, M.A., Maidencombe sowie Marion Horner, M.A., Cambridge
und
Elizabeth Daymond, M.A., Kiel

Beratung:
Maria Büse-Dallmann, Unna; Thomas Denk, Karlsruhe; Ute Fritsch, Ulm; Wolfgang Hamm, Marktredwitz; Sibylle Olms, Everswinkel; Inge Schott, Sennfeld; Elke Weccard, Eislingen; Sabine Weingärtner, Schwäbisch Gmünd; Tanja Wiedmann, Lauffen; Christian Wunsch, M.A., Neumarkt

Visuelle Gestaltung:
Christian Dekelver, Weinstadt; Robert Harvey, London
sowie
Sven Palmowski, Stuttgart

Passend zu diesem Band wird es Tonträger sowie multimediale Lernprogramme geben.

1. Auflage 1 6 5 4 3 2 1 | 2008 2007 2006 2005 2004

Alle Drucke dieser Auflage können im Unterricht nebeneinander benutzt werden.
Die letzte Zahl bezeichnet das Jahr dieses Druckes.

Internetadresse: http://www.klett-verlag.de

Redaktion: Dr. Rudolf Erben (Projektleitung), Ute Erben, Christa Meier, William Sears

Umschlagfotos: Alan Fletcher
Umschlagsgestaltung: AMS Ernst Klett Verlag, Stuttgart
Mediengestaltung: Peter Strinz
Reproduktion: Meyle + Müller, Medien-Management, Pforzheim
Druck: Aprinta, Wemding
ISBN 3-12-582610-1

9 783125 826106

Hallo, willkommen bei *Let's go*

Wir wollen dich durch das Buch begleiten und auch ab und zu ein paar Tipps geben. Damit du dich in deinem Englischbuch zurecht findest, erklären wir dir hier kurz, wie das Buch aufgebaut ist: Es besteht aus Let's start und 7 Kapiteln (Units).

In den Teilen **Language** und **Text** gibt es kleine Texte und Geschichten.
Im Teil **Practice** kannst du üben, was du gelernt hast.
Dann kommen Übungen zu den neuen Wörtern unter der Überschrift **Words**.
Im Teil **Grammar** findest du alles zusammengefasst, was du in dem Kapitel gelernt hast.
Im Teil **Let's check** kannst du mit Hilfe einer Checkliste deinen eigenen Lernfortschritt nachverfolgen.
Die **Bridge**-Seiten zwischen den ersten sechs Units führen thematisch in die neuen Units ein. Gleichzeitig kannst du mit ihnen wiederholen, was du in der Grundschule gelernt hast.

Wenn du ein Wort nicht mehr weißt, kein Problem! Du kannst es in der alphabetischen Wortliste ab Seite 145 nachschlagen. Und da findest du auch Hinweise zur Aussprache, die Zahlen, die Namen und nützliche Sätze, die du im Unterricht brauchst.

TIPP Zum Vokabellernen gibt es auch verschiedene Tipps auf den Words-Seiten.

Du solltest aber auch noch wissen, was die Zeichen vor den Texten und Übungen bedeuten.

Diese Teile gibt es auch auf CD.

Speaking: Übungen zum Sprechen und Zusammenarbeiten

Und jetzt: Let's start! Das heißt: Los geht's (auf Seite 8)!
Viel Spaß beim Englischlernen und bis gleich!

HAPPY BIRTHDAY EMMA

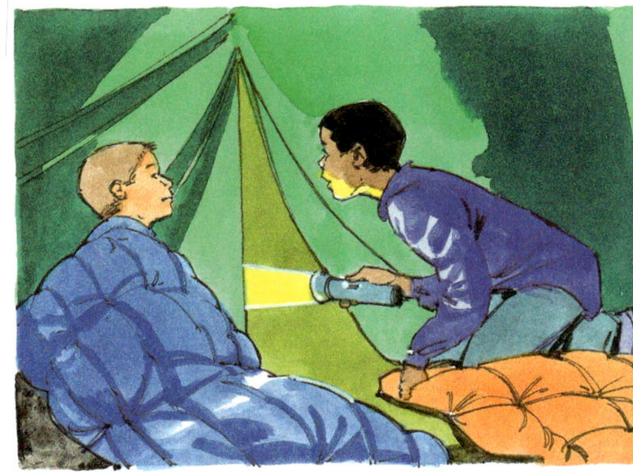

Unit 7 The school year

Extra

Let's start

a This is Greenwich.
Greenwich is in London.

My name is Sam Spencer.
I'm eleven.
I'm from Greenwich.

My name is Tom.
I'm a mouse.
I'm one.
I'm from Greenwich, too.

Say it!

I'm eleven. ***Ich bin** elf.*

1 Sam

Emma: What's your name?
Sam: My name is … .
Emma: How old are you?
Sam: I'm … .
Emma: Where are you from?
Sam: I'm from … .

2 Listening: Emma

What's the right order?

1. My name is Emma Brook.
2. …

Go on, please.

I'm eleven.

I'm from London.

My name is Emma Brook.

I'm new in Greenwich.

3 And you?

1. My name is … .
2. I'm … .
3. I'm from … .

4 A name card

Let's make a card.

5 Listen and speak

1 one 2 two 3 three 4 four

5 five 6 six 7 seven 8 eight

9 nine 10 ten 11 eleven 12 twelve

b

Lisa Taylor is from Greenwich.
She's eleven. She's a chatterbox.

Terry Jackson is a friend.
He's twelve. He's cool.

Sam Spencer is a friend, too.
He's eleven. He's a computer fan.

Emma Brook is a new friend.
She's eleven. She's a music fan.

Say it!

She's a music fan.	***Sie ist** ein Musikfan.*
He's cool.	***Er ist** cool.*

6 He's or she's?

1. Sam:
   He's a boy from Greenwich.
   He's … .
2. Emma: She's … .
   Go on, please.
3. Lisa:
4. Terry:

eleven | cool | twelve | a music fan | a chatterbox | a computer fan | a girl from Greenwich | a boy from Greenwich

7 Speaking: This is Lena

Introduce your friend.

A: Julian, this is Lena. She's eleven.
She's from Stuttgart.
B: Hello, Lena. Nice to meet you.
C: Hello, Julian.

A: Esther, this is … .

Go on, please.

8 What colour?

1. What colour is monster one? – It's yellow.
2. What colour is monster two? – It's … .

Go on, please.

> **Say it!**
> **It's** yellow. ***Es ist** gelb.*

Red, yellow, brown, pink and blue – A big green monster is after you!

9 Speaking: A game

A: ⚂	It's a three.	⚀	a computer fan	⚃	a music fan
B: ⚂	You're cool.	⚁	a chatterbox	⚄	a monster
B: ⚀	It's … .	⚂	cool	⚅	my friend

A: *Go on, please.*

> **Say it!**
> **You're** cool. ***Du bist** cool.*

10 A song: I can sing a rainbow

Red and yellow and pink and green,
Purple and orange and blue.
I can sing a rainbow, sing a rainbow,
Sing a rainbow, too.

Words: Arthur Hamilton

I can sing – *Ich kann singen;*
a rainbow – *ein Regenbogen;*
purple – *lila, violett;* orange – *orange*

Thomas Tallis School

a Thomas Tallis School is in Greenwich. It's a big school.

Everybody in Year 7 is new. Everybody is in uniform.
The Thomas Tallis uniform is blue.

1 That's wrong

1. Thomas Tallis is a shop.
   – That's wrong. Thomas Tallis is a school.
2. Everybody in Year 8 is new.
   – That's wrong. Everybody … .
3. The Thomas Tallis uniform is green. *Go on, please.*
4. Mrs Carter is the caretaker.
5. Mr Newman is a teacher.

b Here are Terry and Sam. They're new at Thomas Tallis, too. They're in Year 7.

Say it!

We're at Thomas Tallis.	***Wir sind*** *in Thomas Tallis.*
You're new here.	***Ihr seid*** *hier neu.*
They're from Greenwich.	***Sie sind*** *aus Greenwich.*

2 Lisa, Emma, Terry and Sam

They're from Greenwich.
They're … .
Go on, please.

new. | in uniform. | from Greenwich. | at Thomas Tallis. | in Year 7.

3 And you?

1. We're from … . 2. We're at … . 3. We're in Year … . 4. We're … .

4 Listening: My new school

What's the right word?

1. I'm at my … school – Thomas Tallis.
2. My new … is cool.
3. My … is blue.
4. Lisa and Sam are …, too.
5. They're … my old school.
6. Thomas Tallis is … .
7. We're in … .

here | uniform | school | new | Year 7 | from | big

c The pupils are in the classroom. They're in tutor group 7MC.

Mrs Carter: Where's Terry Jacks? Are you Terry Jacks?
Terry: No, I'm not. I'm Terry Jackson.
Mrs Carter: Oh, your name is wrong here, Terry. – What's your name?
Sam: Sam Spencer. Oh, my chair.
Mrs Carter: What's wrong? Are you OK, Sam?
Sam: Yes, I am. Thank you, Mrs Carter.
Lisa: He's OK. But not the chair!

Say it!

Are you OK?	***Bist du** OK?*
Yes, I am.	*Ja.*
No, I'm not.	*Nein.*

5 At school

What's missing?

Where's

What's

1. … Thomas Tallis School? – It's in Greenwich.
2 … 7MC? – That's a tutor group in Year 7.
3. … Terry Jackson? – He's in the shop.
4. … everybody? – In the classroom.
5. … wrong? – The name 'Jacks' is wrong.
6. … not OK? – The chair.

6 Speaking: Are you from Greenwich?

Make dialogues with a partner.

A: Are you new here?
B: No, I'm not.
A: Are you …?
Go on, please.

new here? from Greenwich?
from Dortmund? ten?
a computer fan?
a chatterbox?
my friend? …?

d

Say it!

[s]	[z]
one book	one pen
two book**s**	two pen**s**

7 What's in the picture?

Two books …
Go on, please.

8 Your bag

What's in your bag?

9 Speaking: And you?

A: I've got one rubber. And you?
B: I've got … . *Go on, please.*

Say it!

I've got three pencils. ***Ich habe** drei Bleistifte.*

e

Mrs Carter: Is your chair broken, Sam?
Sam: Yes, it is.
Mrs Carter: Let's find Mr Newman.
Lisa: Who's Mr Newman? Is he a teacher?
Mrs Carter: No, he isn't. He's the caretaker.

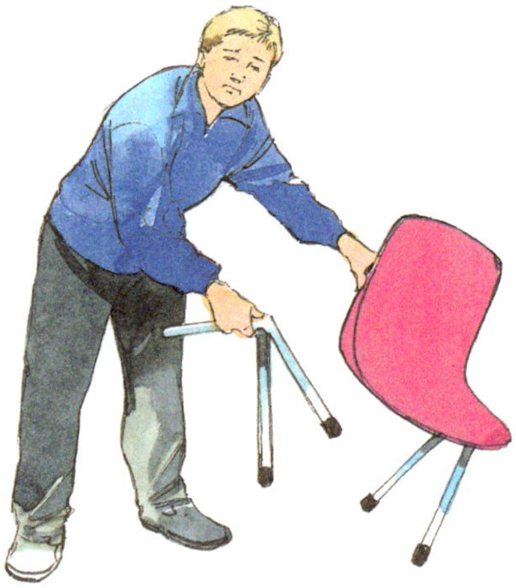

10 Yes and no

1. Is Sam at Thomas Tallis?
   Yes, he is.
2. Is Lisa in Year 8?
   No, she isn't. *Go on, please.*
3. Is the chair broken?
4. Is Emma eleven?
5. Is Terry eleven?
6. Is Mrs Carter a teacher?
7. Is Thomas Tallis in Germany?
8. Is Sam new in Greenwich?
9. Is Lisa in tutor group 7MC?
10. Is the name 'Jackson' wrong?

f Here's a classroom at Thomas Tallis.
The pupils aren't in the classroom.
And the teacher isn't there.

Say it!

The books **aren't** in the bag.
*Die Bücher **sind nicht** in der Tasche.*
The teacher **isn't** there.
*Die Lehrerin **ist nicht** da.*

11 In the classroom

What's in the classroom?

The pink books The blue table …	are is aren't isn't	in the classroom.

12 A song: A rap

A – B – C D E
We're all in 7MC.
F – G – H I J
We're at Thomas Tallis every day.
K – L – M N O
Everybody says hello!
P – Q – R S T
Listen to the ABC!
U V W – X Y Z
Now let's rap the alphabet!

says – *sagt*, rap – *rappen*

13 Spell your name

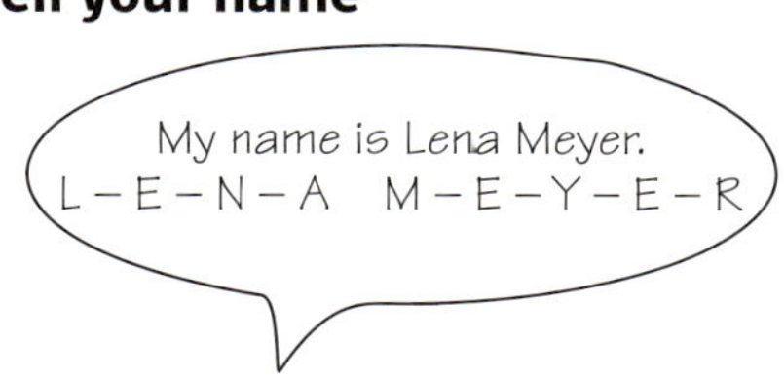

14 Who's your star?

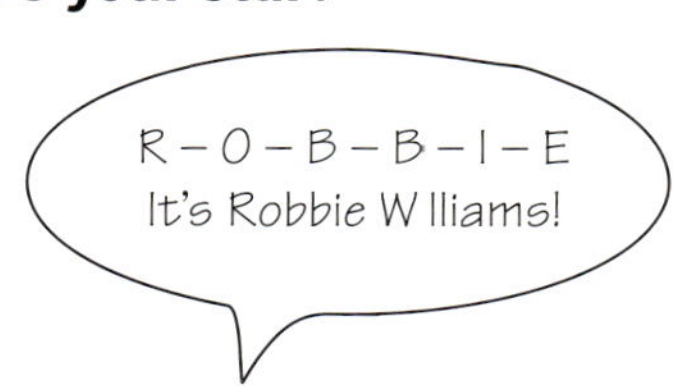

g Thomas Tallis is a modern school.

library

sports hall

cafeteria

shop

computer room

15 In the computer room

The pupils are in the computer room. Here is an e-mail from Terry to a friend.

Hello Eric,
It's cool at Thomas Tallis.
We've got a cafeteria.
We've got a … .
Go on, please.

Say it!

We've got a cafeteria.
***Wir haben** eine Cafeteria.*

16 Listening: Pictures

What's the right picture?

Text 1: That's picture … . Text 2: That's picture … . Text 3: That's picture … .

Friends

It's the lunch break. Emma is with Lisa.

Emma: Here's Terry. He's cool.
Lisa: Cool? He's –
Emma: Sssh!
Terry: Listen, you two. I've got a new joke. What's a word with twenty-six letters?
Emma: That's easy! The word is alphabet! Right?
Terry: Oh. Yes.
Lisa: That isn't a new joke, Terry. It's a boring old joke. All your jokes are boring.
Emma: Lisa! You and Terry are friends.
Terry: No, we aren't. Goodbye, Lisa!

Lisa and Emma are outside now with a ball. Lisa is good at sports. And she's good with a ball. But not Emma.

Emma: Here's the ball, Lisa! Oh no! The ball is in the library.
The girls: Now we've got a problem.

Here are the boys, Sam and Terry.

Sam: Hello. What's the problem?
Emma: It's the ball. It's in the library.
Sam: That's not a problem. The window isn't broken.
Terry: Is it your ball, Emma?
Emma: No, it isn't.
Terry: Oh, is it your ball, Lisa?
Lisa: Yes, it is.
Terry: OK. Your ball – your problem.
Sam: Terry! You and Lisa are friends.
Terry: Friends? No, we aren't. – My jokes are boring.
Lisa: I'm sorry, Terry. Your jokes are OK.
Emma: Please, Terry, the ball.

Terry: Oh, OK. Here you are, Lisa. Sam, let's play.

1 What's the word?

1. defrins: The word is friends.
2. looc: The word is … .
3. ayse: *Go on, please.*
4. borplem
5. lalb
6. kojes

Say it!

That's right.	*Das ist richtig.*
That isn't right.	*Das ist nicht richtig.*

2 Is that right?

1. It's the lunch break.
   – That's right.
2. The joke is a new joke.
   – That isn't right.
3. Lisa and Emma are in the library.
   Go on, please.
4. Lisa is good at sports.
5. Emma is good with a ball.
6. The ball is in the library.
7. The window is broken.
8. Lisa is sorry.

1 Lisa

What's missing?

Lisa: 1. Thomas Tallis School is in Greenwich. … my new school.
2. Emma Brook is new in Greenwich. … my friend now.
3. Sam and Terry are from my old school. … in my tutor group.
4. Sam is a computer fan. … good with computers.
5. The computers here are good. … in the computer room.
6. The sports hall is good, too. … a big sports hall.
7. Mr Newman isn't a teacher. … the caretaker at Thomas Tallis.

She's
He's
They're
It's

2 Hello

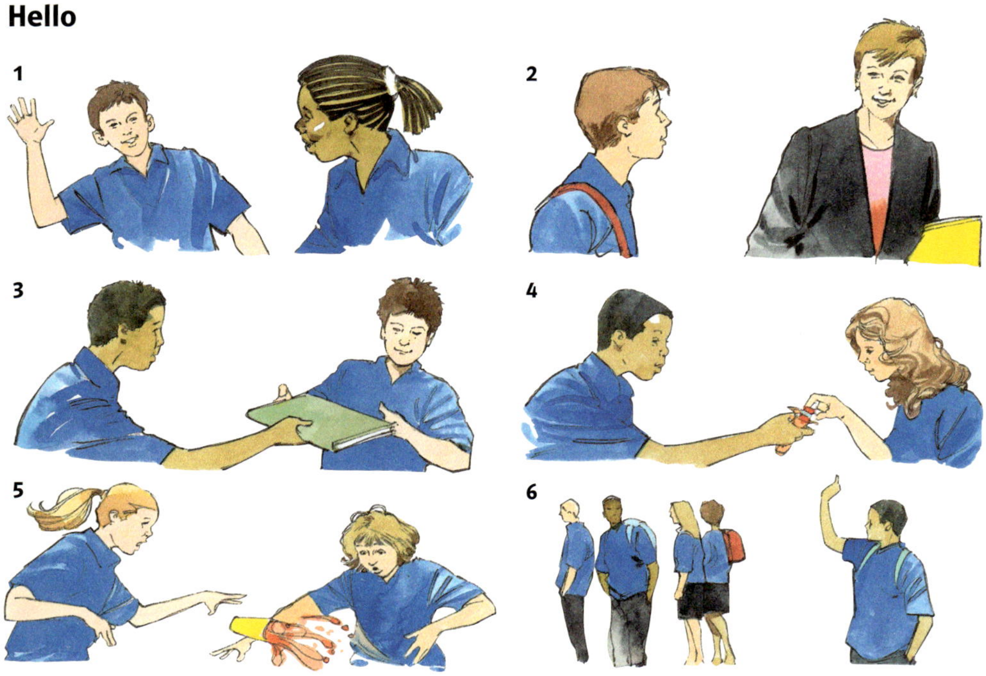

Match the words to the picture.

Picture 1: Hello.
Picture 2: … . *Go on, please.*

Thank you. Here you are.
Goodbye. Oh, I'm sorry. Hello.
Good morning.

3 Speaking: A game

A: What's that?
B: Is it a pen?
A: No, it isn't.
B: Is it a felt-tip?
A: Yes, it is.

Go on, please.

4 At your school

1. Are the classrooms big?
2. Are the chairs OK?
3. Are the books good?
4. Are the pupils in uniform?
5. Are the computers broken?
6. Are the teachers new?

Yes, they are.

No, they aren't.

5 Two pictures

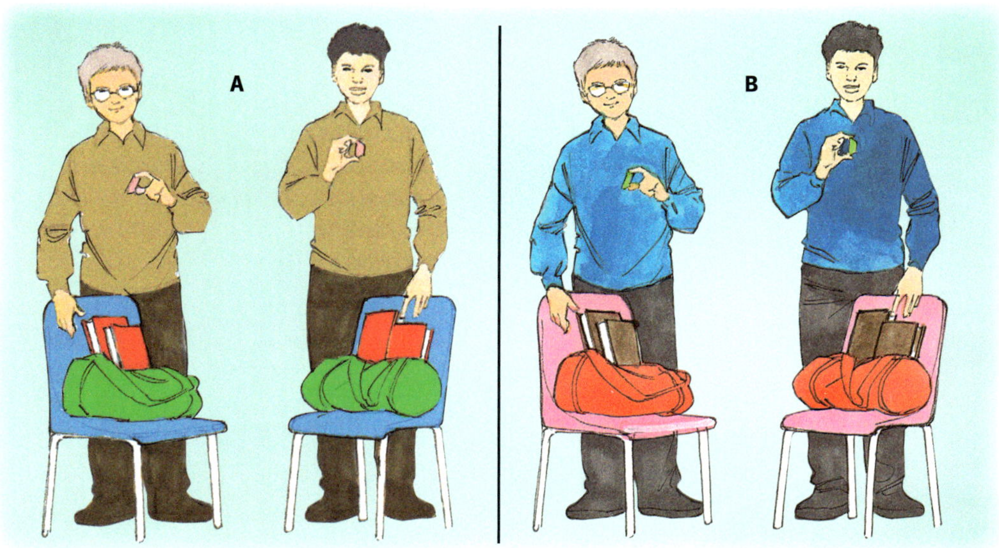

In picture A the uniforms are brown. In picture B the uniforms are blue.
Go on, please.

6 Project: Your school

Make a school poster with pictures and words.

This is .... . | The school is .... . | We've got .... .

Here's .... . | Here are .... . | .... .

TIPP

Tipp: Wörterlernen in Gruppen
Wörter, die zusammengehören, sind leichter zu lernen. Gewöhne dich daran, Wörter in Gruppen zu sammeln. Trage sie in einer Liste oder in einem Wortnetz (word web) zusammen. Später kannst du neue Wörter dazuschreiben. Wie das geht, lernst du in den Übungen 7, 8 und 9.

7 Word lists

Make two lists with the words.

who?	where?
girl	classroom
…	…

girl classroom boy library partner
computer room teacher cafeteria caretaker outside
everybody friend shop sports hall pupil

8 Word groups

Make two groups.
Find names for the groups.

book red ruler felt-tip yellow rubber
green pen brown pink pencil case blue

9 A word web

a) *Here's a word web.*

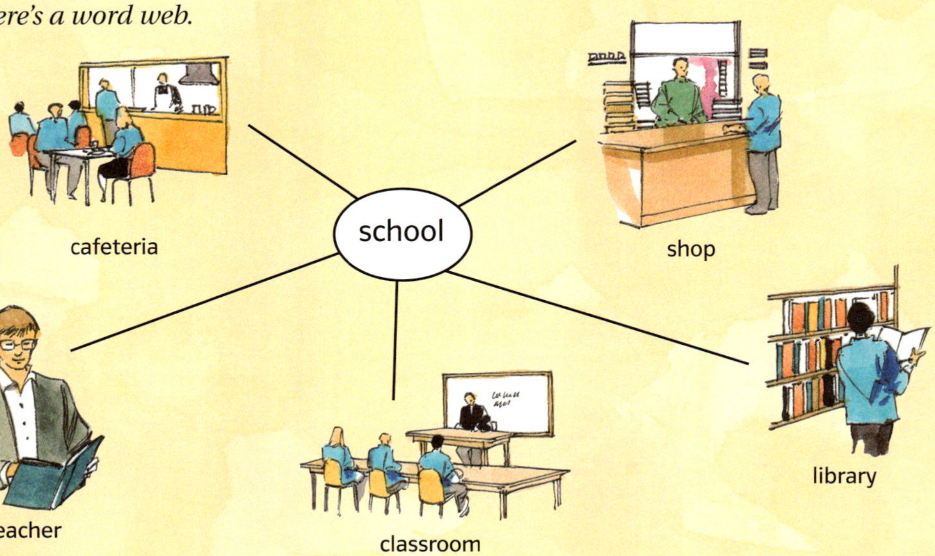

b) *Make a word web for 'in my bag' in your exercise book.*

10 Listen and speak

Make two lists with the words.

words	shops	letters	sports
balls	groups	boys	names
lists	bags	books	jokes

[z]	[s]
one word two words	one shop two shops

11 Picture words

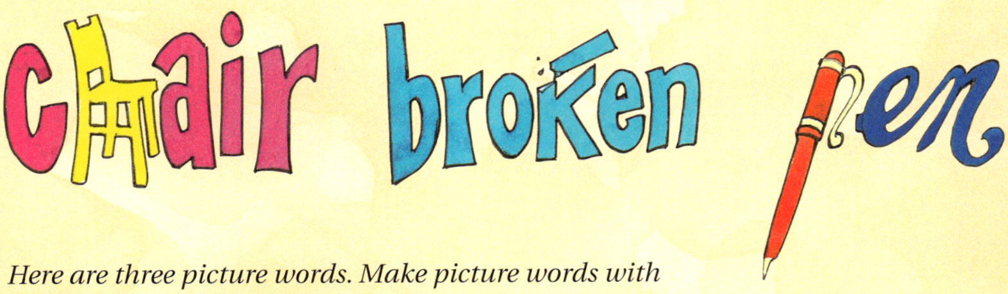

Here are three picture words. Make picture words with the words 'pencil', 'sports' and 'ball'.

12 Speaking: What's in your school bag?

A: In my school bag I've got a pen.
B: In my school bag I've got a pen and a rubber.
C: In my school bag I've got a pen and a rubber and a … .
Go on, please.

13 Words

What are the words in the picture?
yes, girl …
Go on, please.

be *(sein)*

• am, are

Aussage	**I'm** eleven.	***Ich bin** elf.*
Verneinung	**I'm not** ten.	***Ich bin nicht** zehn.*
Ja/Nein-Frage	**Are you** eleven? **– Yes, I am.** **– No, I'm not.**	***Bist du** elf?* ***– Ja.*** ***– Nein.***
wh-Frage	Where **are you?**	*Wo **bist du?***

• is

Aussage	**She's** new here.	***Sie ist** neu hier.*
Verneinung	**He isn't** new here.	***Er ist nicht** neu hier.*
Ja/Nein-Frage	**Is he** new here? **– Yes, he is.** **– No, he isn't.**	***Ist er** neu hier?* ***– Ja.*** ***– Nein.***
wh-Frage	Where **is she?**	*Wo **ist sie?***

a/the *(Artikel)*

Terry's got **a** joke.	*Terry hat **einen** Witz.*
The joke isn't new.	***Der** Witz ist nicht neu.*

Plural *(Mehrzahl)*

[z]	[s]
pen – pens	book – books
bag – bags	felt-tip – felt-tips
boy – boys	shop – shops

Schau, ganz einfach: In der Mehrzahl hat das Hauptwort meist ein -s.

Cartoon: Is he new here?

Checklist

Ich kann
... sagen, wie ich heiße.
... sagen, woher ich komme.
... meine Telefonnummer sagen.
... jemanden fragen, wie er heißt.
... jemanden fragen, wie alt er ist.
... jemanden fragen, woher er kommt.
... jemanden nach der Telefonnummer fragen.
... jemanden vorstellen.
... Auskunft über meine Schule geben.
... sagen, dass etwas richtig oder falsch ist.
... sagen, dass mir etwas Leid tut.
... etwas anbieten und mich bedanken.
... jemanden begrüßen und mich verabschieden.
Und ich weiß, dass man nicht nur mit „Yes" oder „No" antwortet.

My name is ... . (*Oder:* I'm ... .)
I'm from ... .
My telephone number is ... .
What's your name?
How old are you?
Where are you from?
What's your telephone number?

This is ... . She's from ... .
We've got a cafeteria.
That's right./That's wrong.

Oh, sorry. (*Oder:* I'm sorry.)
Here you are./Thank you.
Hello./Goodbye.

Are you from Germany?
– Yes, I am.

Checkout: Australia

Teacher: Tommy, which is further away – Australia or the moon?
Tommy: Australia, Sir.
Teacher: Australia? Why?
Tommy: Because you can see the moon, but you can't see Australia.

In diesem Witz sind einige Wörter, die du nicht kennst. Versuche, den Witz zu verstehen. Einige Wörter kannst du raten oder aus dem Zusammenhang erschließen, andere in der alphabetischen Wortliste ab Seite 145 nachschlagen.

TIPP

Tipps: Australia
1. further away: *Schau dir die Pfeile in der Abbildung an.* Further away *ist der Ort, auf den der längere Pfeil zeigt.*
2. Australia: *Das deutsche Wort ist so ähnlich wie im Englischen.*
3. because: *Mit diesem Wort erklärt man, warum etwas ist.*

A house for a mouse

1. bathroom
2. bedroom
3. kitchen
4. dining room
5. living room
6. table
7. chair
8. TV
9. picture
10. bed
11. sofa
12. cupboard
13. cheese
14. game
15. cat
16. rucksack

1. Tom is in his new house. What are the rooms?
   A bedroom, a … . *Go on, please.*
2. What colour are the rooms? *Make dialogues.*
3. *Listen.* Where's Tom?
   Tom is in … . Now he's in … . *Go on, please.*

Speaking

What colour is the kitchen?

It's yellow.

What colour …?

Go on, please.

Where's the table?

The table is here.

Where's …?

Go on, please.

4. What's in the van?
   A sofa, a … . *Go on, please.*
5. Where is it? *Make dialogues.*
6. *Listen to the mouse rap.* Can you say it?
7. What's in the rucksack?
   Cheese, … . *Go on, please.*

Mouse rap

Hello, I'm Tom
and that's my bedroom,
with my table, chairs and bed.
Blue TV and yellow cupboard
and my big new sofa, red.

At home

Say it!

The Brooks **have got** a flat.
*Die Brooks **haben** eine Wohnung.*
They **haven't got** a house.
*Sie **haben** kein Haus.*

a **The Jacksons**

This is Terry's house in Hither Farm Road. They've got a big garden with trees. Terry's shed is in the garden – a cool meeting place for the friends.

The Brooks

Emma: Here's my family: my mother, my father and my sister Nasreen. We haven't got a house or a garden. We've got a flat over the shop.

1 That's wrong

1. Terry's house is in Greenwich Road. That's wrong. It's in … . *Go on, please.*
2. Terry's house is a good meeting place.
3. Nina is Emma's sister.
4. Emma's mother and father have got a garden.
5. Sam's flat is in Hither Farm Road.
6. Sam's mother and father are in the picture, too.
7. Lisa's sister is Nasreen.
8. Lisa, Jade and Ben haven't got a dog.

2 The friends

1. Mr Jackson is … father.
2. … flat is in Wendover Road.
3. Emma is … sister.
4. … shed is in the garden.
5. Ben is … brother.
6. … grandma is in the picture, too.
7. … father and mother have got a shop.
8. Jade is … sister.

Sam's (2 x) | Lisa's (2 x) | Terry's (2 x) | Emma's | Nasreen's

The Taylors

This is Lisa's flat and family. Jade is Lisa's sister and Ben is Lisa's brother. They've got a dog, Barker.

The Spencers

Sam: This is my family. Here's my grandma and my father. We've got a flat in Wendover Road. We haven't got a car.

3 The Jacksons and the Brooks

The Jacksons	have got	a house.
The Brooks	haven't got	a flat.
		a garden.
		a shop.
		a shed.
		a dog.

The Jacksons have got a house.
Go on, please.

4 Listening: Four families

Who is it?

Text 1: That's the … .
Go on, please.

Jacksons | Taylors
Brooks | Spencers

b It's Friday after school.
Terry is at home. Lisa and Emma are there, too.
They're in the garden.

Emma: Have you got brothers and sisters?
Terry: No, I haven't.
Emma: And you?
Lisa: Yes, I have. I've got a brother and a sister.

Say it!
Have you **got** a brother?
***Hast** du einen Bruder?*
Yes, I have. *Ja.*
No, I haven't. *Nein.*

5 Speaking: Brothers and sisters

a) *Act the dialogue with a partner.*

b) *Ask your friends.*
A: Have you got ...?
B: ... .
Go on, please.

6 Speaking: What have you got?

Ask the class.

Go on, please.

c Emma's flat is small. She's got a room with Nasreen.
Emma hasn't got her own room.
She's tidy. But Nasreen isn't tidy.

Say it!
She**'s got** a room.
Sie ***hat*** ein Zimmer.
She **hasn't got a** ball.
Sie ***hat keinen*** Ball.

7 Emma and Nasreen

Say what they've got or haven't got.

Emma
1. Emma has got books.
2. Emma has got … .
3. Emma hasn't got … .

Nasreen
1. Nasreen has … .
Go on, please.

d
Mrs Brook: Has Terry got a nice room?
Emma: Yes, he has. And he's got a cool shed.
Mrs Brook: A cool shed?
Emma: It's a great meeting place. He's got crazy things there.

Say it!
Has he **got** a nice room?
Hat *er ein schönes Zimmer?*

8 Friends and family

1. Has Terry got a cool shed?
   – Yes, he has.
2. Has Lisa got two brothers?
   – No, she hasn't.
3. Has Nasreen got …?
   Go on, please.

1. Terry – a cool shed?
2. Lisa – two brothers?
3. Nasreen – her own room?
4. Mrs Brook – a flat?
5. Mr Brook – a computer shop?
6. Lisa – a dog?
7. Emma – a radio?

e Emma's mother is from India.
Her name is Farah.
She's a nurse.

Say it!

Her father is English.
__Ihr__ Vater ist Engländer.
His shop is in Greenwich.
__Sein__ Geschäft ist in Greenwich.

Her father is English.
His name is Rob.
His computer shop is in Holburn Road.

9 Speaking: Friends

a) *Who is it?*

She's a girl.
Her mother is a nurse.
Her father is English.
Her sister is Nasreen.
What's her name?
Her name is … .

b) *Talk about a friend.*

He's a boy.
His friends are … .
His teacher is … .
His flat is in … .
What's his name?
His name is … .

f The friends are in the shed.
It's fun at the meeting place.
They can read comics.
They can watch cartoons.
They can listen to music or play Terry's drums.
They can have a party and do crazy things.

Say it!

They **can** listen to music.
Sie __können__ Musik hören.

10 And you?

What can you do at home?

I can read comics.
I can … .
Go on, please.

read
listen to
watch
play
have

a party
books
CDs
TV
cartoons
comics
a game
the radio
…

11 Mr Brook

Mr Brook isn't at home on Sunday.
He's in the shop.

He can't listen to CDs.
He can't read … .
He can't watch … . *Go on, please.*

12 Speaking: Breakfast

Make breakfast dialogues with a partner.

A: Tea ?
B: Yes, please.
A: Can you give me the butter, please?
B: Here you are.
A: Thank you.

Yes, please.

No, thank you.

13 In the kitchen

The Brooks are at the breakfast table.
What's missing?

I'm | we're | it's | they're | she's | you're | he's

1. *Mrs Brook:* Where's your father?
   Emma: … in the shop.
2. *Mrs Brook:* Is Nasreen in the shop, too?
   Emma: No, … in bed.
3. *Mrs Brook:* Oh, here's Nasreen.
   Nasreen: Yes, … here now.
4. *Nasreen:* Where are the cornflakes?
   Emma: … here.
5. *Mrs Brook:* Is your toast OK?
   Emma: Yes, … good. Thank you.
6. *Nasreen:* Emma, this is my toast.
   Emma: No, it isn't. … awful, Nasreen.
7. *Mrs Brook:* Please, girls!
   Nasreen: I'm sorry. … friends now. Right, Emma?

14 Listening: Three flats and a house

1. Have the Brooks got a garden?
2. Where can Terry play?
3. Have the Taylors got a flat?
4. What has Mr Spencer got?

The room

1. It's Saturday. Lisa is with Emma in Emma's flat. Where can they play? Nasreen is in the bedroom with a friend. They're on the bed.

2. The room is a problem on Sunday, too. Emma has got a new CD. But Nasreen has got homework. She can't do her homework with Emma's music.

3. Emma can play her CD in the living room. That's OK with her father. But it isn't OK with Emma. She's angry. She hasn't got her own room.

4. Emma is at Terry's house in the shed. She isn't happy. But she can talk about the problem with her room. Maybe Terry can help. It's fun in the shed. Emma is happy again.

5. Mr and Mrs Brook are worried. Where's Emma? Oh, she's here. The problems with the room can't go on. Nasreen has got an idea.

6. Nasreen's idea is rules for the room. Emma and Nasreen can make the rules. Two sisters in one room – that isn't easy!

1 Cool music!

Match the words to the people.

1. Cool music!
   – That's Emma.
2. We've got the room.
   – That's … . *Go on, please.*
3. It's awful here.
4. Let's talk.
5. You're lucky.
6. We've got a small flat.

2 They've got the room

Picture 1: Have Nasreen and her friend got the room?
– Yes, they have.
Picture 2: Has Emma got homework?
– *Go on, please.*
Picture 3: Has Emma got her own room?
Picture 4: Has Terry got a big sister?
Picture 5: Have Mr and Mrs Brook got an idea?
Picture 6: Have Emma and Nasreen got rules for the room?

1 Six pictures

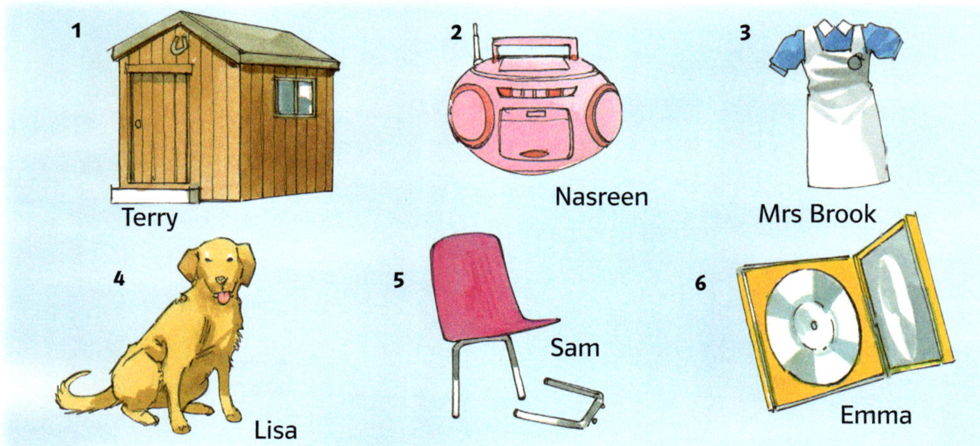

Picture 1: That's Terry's shed.
Go on, please.

Picture 2: That's … . *Go on, please.*

2 What's the right word?

1. You've got a nice room. … bed is cool.
2. My father has got a shop. He has got computers in … shop.
3. I've got a dog. He's … friend.
4. My sister has got a cupboard. But … things are on the bed.
5. A boy at school has got a new skateboard.
   … skateboard is new, too.
6. I've got a big table. But … table isn't tidy.
7. She has got a sister. … sister is five.
8. You've got my pen. That isn't … pen.

my
your
her
his

3 Speaking: In the classroom

Make dialogues with a partner.

A: I haven't got a red felt-tip.
B: Here's my red felt-tip.
A: Thank you.

A: I haven't got … .
Go on, please.

rubber ruler pen pencil
pencil case book …

4 No!

1. *Pupil:* Cats are awful.
   Class: No, they aren't.
2. *Pupil:* You're a teacher.
   Class: No, I'm not.
3. *Pupil:* The room is OK.
   Class: No, it … .
4. *Pupil:* Your sister is tidy.
   Class: No, … .
5. *Pupil:* School is boring.
   Class: No, … .
6. *Pupil:* Cornflakes are nice.
   Class: No, … .
7. *Pupil:* Terry is old.
   Class: No, … .
8. *Pupil:* You're crazy.
   Class: No, … .

5 Speaking: Can you do it?

a) *Look at the ideas and write questions.*

make: a game/eggs/a poster/…
draw: Tom/a shed/your teacher/…
play: football/the drums/…
read: a cartoon in English/ a boring book/…

	Patrick	Nadine
Can you make eggs?	–	…
Can you draw Tom?	+	
Can you play football?	+	

b) *Ask your friend the questions.*

Yes, I can. No, I can't.

A: Can you make eggs, Patrick?
B: No, I can't.
A: Can you draw pictures?
B: Yes, I can.
A: Can you … ? *Go on, please.*

c) *Say what your friend can do.*

Patrick can't make eggs.
He can draw pictures.
Go on, please.

Nadine can … .
She can't … . *Go on, please.*

6 Project: Your room

What's in your room?
Make a poster.

TIPP

Tipp: Wörterlernen durch Bilder
Nutze dein „Bildgedächtnis" und arbeite so viel wie möglich mit Bildern. Viele Vokabeln bezeichnen Gegenstände. Zeichne sie oder schneide Bilder aus und klebe sie in dein Vokabelheft. Sprich die englischen Wörter dann mehrmals nacheinander. Du kannst es am Beispiel des Wortnetzes in Übung 7 ausprobieren.

7 Word web: Breakfast

Make a word web for 'breakfast' in your exercise book.

8 What can you do in your room?

a) *Make questions.*

1. Can you play the drums?
2. *Go on, please.*

Can you	have	crazy things?
	make	TV?
	read	homework?
	watch	a game?
	play	breakfast?
	do	the radio?
	listen to	a book?
		a party?

b) *Now answer the questions.*

A: Can you play the drums?
B: No, I can't.
A: Can you … ?
B: Go on, please.

9 Listen and speak: Say it in English

ball – butter – CD – name – problem – TV – radio – poster – uniform

10 How many can you find?

1. Eight houses.
2. … cars.

Go on, please.

- house
- car
- skateboard
- shop
- cat
- tree

11 Picture words

Here are more picture words. Make picture words with the words 'angry', 'idea' and 'milk'.

12 Speaking: A game

A: What's this?
B: Is it a ball?
A: No, it isn't.
B: Is it an apple?
A: Yes. Right.

Say it!

a ball	***ein*** *Ball*
an apple	***ein*** *Apfel*

have got (haben, besitzen)

• have got

Aussage	I've **got** a dog.	***Ich habe*** *einen Hund.*
Verneinung	**I haven't got** a dog.	***Ich habe keinen*** *Hund.*
Ja/Nein-Frage	**Have you got** a dog? **– Yes, I have.** **– No, I haven't.**	***Hast du*** *einen Hund?* ***– Ja.*** ***– Nein.***
wh-Frage	What **have you got** there?	*Was **hast du** da?*

• has got

Aussage	**She's got** a sister.	***Sie hat*** *eine Schwester.*
Verneinung	**He hasn't got** a brother.	***Er hat keinen*** *Bruder.*

can (können)

Aussage	**I can** play the drums.	***Ich kann*** *Schlagzeug spielen.*
Verneinung	**He can't** draw a dog.	***Er kann keinen*** *Hund malen.*
Ja/Nein-Frage	**Can you** play football? – **Yes, I can.** – **No, I can't.**	***Kannst du*** *Fußball spielen?* ***– Ja.*** ***– Nein.***
wh-Frage	Where **can we** have a party?	*Wo **können wir** eine Party machen?*

Genitive (Genitiv – besitzanzeigendes s)

Jade is Lisa**'s** sister.
Jade ist Lisas Schwester.

Das ist kinderleicht. Deutsch und Englisch sind hier fast gleich bis auf eine Kleinigkeit.

Cartoon: I can play the drums.

Checklist

Ich kann	
… sagen, was ich habe.	I've got a dog.
… sagen, was ich nicht habe.	I haven't got a house.
… jemanden fragen, ob er etwas hat.	Have you got a brother?
… sagen, welche Nationalität jemand hat.	Her father is English.
… sagen, welchen Beruf jemand hat.	She's a nurse.
… sagen, was ich zu Hause tun kann.	I can watch TV.
… sagen, was ich zu Hause nicht tun kann.	I can't play the drums.
… jemanden fragen, was er kann.	Can you play football?
… jemanden um etwas bitten.	Can you give me the butter, please?

Checkout: Welcome to Brook Park

1. You can play football here.
2. This is the meeting place for dogs. Bring your dog, too!
3. Here's the kiosk. We've got sandwiches, chocolate and drinks.
4. Please!
   No loud music.
   No bikes.
   No rubbish.
   You can put your old paper and your drink cans in here.

Was kann man in Brook Park alles tun? Was sollte man lieber lassen? Hier gibt es wieder einige Wörter oder Wendungen, die du nicht kennst. Du kannst sie in der alphabetischen Wortliste nachschlagen oder aus dem Zusammenhang erschließen.

TIPP

Tipps: Welcome to Brook Park

1. Bring your dog: Bring *ist eine Aufforderung. Die deutsche Übersetzung ist fast wie im Englischen.*
2. kiosk, chocolate: *Die deutschen Wörter sind so ähnlich wie die englischen.*
3. No bikes/No rubbish: *Schau dir die Abbildungen an und es ist klar, was gemeint ist.*

Hobbies

1. basketball
2. the guitar
3. tennis
4. rabbit
5. frog
6. fish
7. guinea pig
8. bird
9. favourite

1. What can Tom play?
   Tom can play games. He … .
2. *Make dialogues about Tom.*
3. Tom has got a poster with animals.
   What are the animals?
   A cat, a … .

Mouse rap

Tom, the mouse,
is in the house
with his friend, the cat.
She isn't fat.
The fish are cool,
they're in the pool.

fat – *fett*; pool – *Schwimmbecken*

Speaking

Can Tom play the drums?

Yes, he can.

Can Tom …?

Go on, please.

Is your favourite pet a fish?

No, it isn't.

Is your favourite pet …?

Go on, please.

4. Tom's favourite animal is the cat.
   What's your favourite animal? *Make dialogues.*
5. *Listen to the mouse rap.* Can you say it?
6. Where's Susie?
7. What's in the rucksack? What's missing?

Fun with the friends

a

Say it!

I **play** basketball on Monday.
*Ich **spiele** am Montag Basketball.*

1 Hobbies

a) *Match the parts of the sentences.*

1. I go swimming	at the weekend.
2. I play for	on Friday.
3. I watch	the school basketball team.
4. We train	on Tuesday.
5. We sing and dance	to boy bands with my friends.
6. I go jogging	on Monday and Thursday.
7. We practise	Formula One on TV.
8. I listen	with my dog.

b) *Look at the sentences again.*
Who is it?

Number 1: That's Lisa.
Go on, please.

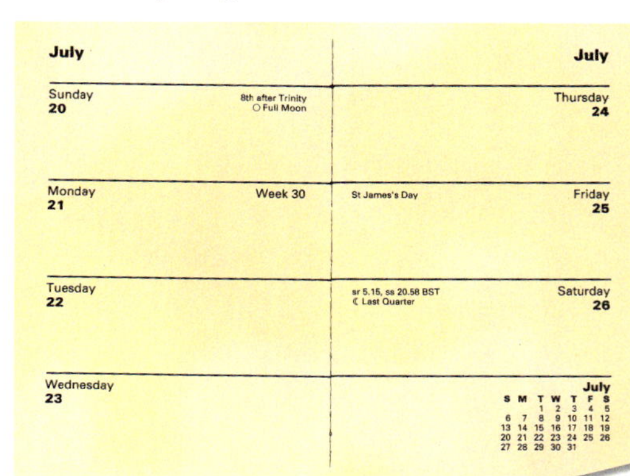

Say it!

We **practise** at the weekend.
*Wir **üben** am Wochenende.*

2 And you?

Talk about your hobbies.

I play
I go
I read
I listen to
I do
I watch
I …

…

on Monday.
on Tuesday.
on Wednesday.
on Thursday.
on Friday.
on Saturday.
on Sunday.
at the weekend.

3 Listening: At the weekend

Say what Nasreen and Ben do.

	Saturday	Sunday
Nasreen	…………	…………
Ben	…………	…………

b Sam is with his cousin, Dan.

Dan: I work at Galaxy Radio now. Young people always listen to my programme. You can listen to my programme from Monday to Friday. I never work on Saturday or Sunday.
Sam: Is the programme fun?
Dan: Yes, it is. I always play cool music, and I sometimes talk to pop stars. My fans send me e-mails every day. They often phone me, too, and we talk on the programme. We sometimes talk about problems, and we often do a quiz or play a game.
Sam: Can I be on Galaxy Radio, too?

Say it!

They **always** listen to my programme.
*Sie hören **immer** meine Sendung.*
Fans **often** phone me.
*Fans rufen mich **oft** an.*
I **always** play cool music.
*Ich spiele **immer** coole Musik.*
I **never** work on Saturday.
*Ich arbeite **nie** am Samstag.*

4 Dan's programme

What's the right order? Make sentences.

1. always/young people/my programme/listen to
   Young people always listen to my programme.
2. or Sunday/never work/I/on Saturday
3. phone me/often/too/they
4. talk/on the programme/we
5. about problems/talk/sometimes/we
6. a quiz/we/often/do
7. always/I/cool music/play
8. sometimes/pop stars/I/talk to

5 Speaking: You and your friends

a) *Talk with a partner. Say what you do.*

I always I often I sometimes I never	send e-mails. phone friends. talk to pop stars. play the drums. listen to cool music. sing karaoke. dance with friends. do homework. watch TV.

b) *Now say what you and your partner do.*
We always … . We often … .
Go on, please.

c Sam always talks to Dan on Saturday. Sometimes Emma goes with him. Today Sam and Emma have got a survey for Dan. It's about music.
Dan: That's cool! Let's talk about the survey on Galaxy Radio.

+++	always	+	sometimes
++	often	–	never

	Emma	Sam	Terry	Lisa	Ben	Nasreen
buys CDs	+	–	++	+	++	++
sings karaoke	++	–	–	–	–	–
goes to crazy parties	+	+	–	+	+++	+
listens to Galaxy Radio	+++	+++	+	–	++	++

6 The friends

Look at the survey. Then talk about the friends.

1. Emma sometimes buys CDs.
   She often … .
2. Sam never buys … . *Go on, please.*

Say it!

She sometimes buy**s** CDs.
***Sie kauft** manchmal CDs.*
He never go**es** to parties.
***Er geht** nie auf Partys.*

7 Speaking: A game

Play a game with the words 'always', 'often', 'sometimes' and 'never'.

d It's Monday. Dan is at Galaxy Radio.

Dan: Hi, this is Galaxy Dan, your number 1 DJ.
Who's our caller, please?
Katie: Hello, Dan. My name is Katie.
Dan: Hi, Katie, where are you from?
Katie: I'm from Greenwich.
Dan: Oh, that's very nice.
What can I play for you?
Katie: Can you play the song 'Our House' for my friends in London?
It's their favourite song.
Dan: OK, Katie, here's the song.

Say it!

Your number 1 DJ.	***Euer*** *DJ Nummer 1.*
Who's **our** caller?	*Wer ist* ***unser*** *Anrufer?*
Their song.	***Ihr*** *Lied.*

8 Our song

What's missing?

our | your | their

1. *Dan:* OK, fans, here's … number 1 DJ.
2. *Katie's friends:* That's … song on Galaxy Radio!
3. *Dan:* Young people often talk to me about … problems.
4. *Katie:* My friends are happy! … song is on Galaxy Radio.
5. *Dan:* Phone me on Monday and I can play … favourite song.
6. *Dan:* Pop stars never talk to me about … problems.
7. *Katie's friends:* Galaxy Dan is … favourite DJ now.

9 Speaking: Your DJ dialogue

a) *Make your own DJ dialogue with a partner.* b) *Now act the dialogue.*

Let's start!	What can you ask?	What can you say after that?
This is … .	Where are you from?	Here' s your song.
Hello, here's … .	Who's our caller, please?	Here's a great song for Paul from Essen.
I'm your crazy DJ … .	Can you say that again, please?	Here's a new song from the Blue Monsters.
Hi, friends, … .	What can I play for you?	Goodbye!
	Who are your friends?	
	What's their favourite song?	

e Lisa and Barker are in the park. There is a man with balloons in the park. There are four girls with a ball, too. That's nice for Barker!

10 What's in the park?

1. There is a man with balloons.
2. There are four girls with a ball.
3. There … . *Go on, please.*

Say it!

There is a man.	***Da ist*** *ein Mann.*
There are four girls.	***Da sind*** *vier Mädchen.*

11 Numbers

a) *Can you find the numbers?*

2: two	3: three	4: four
12: twelve	13: …	14: …
20: …	30: …	40: …

b) *What's missing?*

1. two, three, four, five, …
2. thirteen, fourteen, fifteen, …
3. twenty-nine, thirty, thirty-one, …
4. twenty-two, thirty-two, forty-two, …
5. sixty-five, seventy-five, eighty-five, …
6. twenty-five, fifty, seventy-five, …

12 Listening: Bingo

a) *Write six numbers from one to fifty. Listen for your numbers.*

b) *Now write six numbers from fifty-one to one hundred. Listen for your numbers.*

Barker's story

Hello. I'm Barker.

My family are the Taylors – Richard and Susan Taylor and their children Lisa, Ben and Jade. I help the Taylors. That's my job.

Lisa is my pet.
In the morning I get up and I wash her face.
Then she washes her face again and we have breakfast.
Toast!

After school I go to the park. I take Lisa and Jade with me.
They often play there with their friends. I play, too. I always take their ball. That's fun!
Sometimes they get lost in the park.
Then they call my name.
I always find the friends, and then we go home.

In the evening we often watch TV.
Then we play a game.
I sit in front of the TV and the Taylors throw their shoes.
That's fun! I like shoes.

On Sundays I go out with my family in the car.
There are always cars on the road.
Sometimes there are dogs in the cars.
I bark and they bark, too.
That's great.

After a long day Lisa is tired.
We go to bed.
Lisa is my friend.
She can sleep with me.
She's always dog-tired.

1 Barker the dog

Talk about Barker.

He	helps	with Lisa and her friends.
	washes	the friends in the park.
	gets up	the family.
	plays	on Lisa's bed.
	finds	and the dogs bark, too.
	sits	in the morning.
	barks	Lisa's face.
	sleeps	in front of the TV.

2 When is it?

1. They go to the park.
   That's after school.
2. They watch TV.
   That's … . *Go on, please.*
3. They wash their faces.
4. They're tired.
5. They go out in the car.

1 Tom's Friday

sometimes/go jogging

sleep/in the lunch break

always/sing karaoke

never/watch TV

often/practise card tricks

have breakfast/in the evening

Look at the pictures.
Then talk about Tom's Friday.

1. Tom sometimes goes jogging.
2. He … . *Go on, please.*

2 Speaking: Who is it?

Make cards. Write five sentences about you.
Put the cards together. Take one and read the sentences. Who is it?

I'm a boy.
I like computers.
I often watch Formula One on TV.
I sometimes read comics.
I never sing.

A: I think that's Marco.
He likes computers.
B: No, that's wrong. It isn't Marco.
C: Is it Daniel?
He often watches Formula One.
D: That's right. It's Daniel.

3 Project: Pets in your class

a) Who has got a pet in your class?
Ask your friends. Make a list.

b) *Talk about it in class.*
Six pupils have got dogs.
Eight pupils have got … .

dogs ~~||||~~ |
cats ~~||||~~ |||

4 Speaking: A new player

It's the lunch break.
A new player is with Terry.

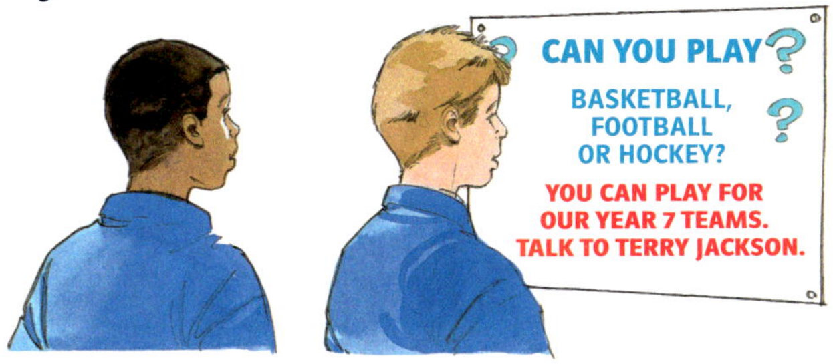

a) *Act the dialogue with a partner.*

b) *Make new dialogues.*

New player: Hi. Are you Terry Jackson?
Terry: Yes, I am.
New player: Can I play basketball with your team?
Terry: Yes, you can. Are you a good player?
New player: Yes, I am.
Terry: We always train on Monday.
New player: Great.
Terry: We train after school, at the sports hall.
New player: Cool. See you there.
Terry: OK. Bye!

football
hockey

Tuesday
Wednesday
Thursday

in the lunch break
in the evening

5 At a basketball game

There is a basketball game on Sunday.
What can you see in the sports hall?

the basketball team · the fans · a dog · a new player · the new teacher · Ben · Galaxy Dan · Terry and Emma

1. Look. There is the basketball team.
2. Look. There are … .
   Go on, please.

TIPP

Tipp: Wörterlernen mit dem Wandkalender
Nimm einen alten Wandkalender und hänge ihn mit der Bildseite zur Wand in deinem Zimmer auf. Schreibe alle Wörter darauf, die du dir nicht merken kannst. Streiche nach und nach die Wörter aus, die du inzwischen kennst. Du kannst mit den Wörtern auf dieser Seite anfangen.

6 Word web: Hobbies

Make a word web in your exercise book for 'hobbies'.

7 Listen and speak

Make three groups with the words.

dances – does – finds – gives – goes – likes – listens – phones – plays – practises – gets – sings – spells – starts – takes – talks – washes – thinks – trains – watches – works

[-s]	[-z]	[-ɪz]
likes	does	dances

8 Small words

What's missing?

after at for in on with

1. Emma dances with her friends … Friday.
2. Dan never works … the weekend.
3. Sam does card tricks … his father.
4. Tom always sleeps … the lunch break.
5. The pupils train … school.
6. Terry plays … the basketball team.

9 Yes and no

Make pairs.

yes	always	big	wrong	young	here
never	no	old	right	there	small

1. yes – no
2. *Go on, please.*

10 A poem: Playing with words

You can play with dice
You can play with cards
You can play with a ball
You can play with words
words
words
words
words
words
banana
words
words
words
words
words

Michael Rosen

poem – *Gedicht*; dice – *Würfel*; banana – *Banane*

11 Picture words

Here are more picture words. Make picture words with the words 'balloon', 'shoe' and 'song'.

12 A game

Find a word and write it down.
Your partner starts with the last letter
and makes a new word.
Go on, please.

Present simple *(einfache Gegenwart)*

- present simple mit *I*

Aussage	**I play** basketball on Friday.	***Ich spiele*** *Basketball am Freitag.*
	I sometimes play the drums.	***Ich spiele manchmal*** *Schlagzeug.*
	I never work on Sunday.	***Ich arbeite nie*** *am Sonntag.*

- present simple mit *he/she*

He, she, it, *das „s" muss mit!*

Aussage	**She often phones** friends.	***Sie ruft oft*** *Freunde an.*
	He always goes to parties.	***Er geht immer*** *auf Partys.*

Achtung: go → goes; watch → watches

Possessive pronouns *(besitzanzeigende Fürwörter)*

This is **my** book.	*Dies ist **mein** Buch.*
Is she **your** sister?	*Ist sie **deine** Schwester?*
What's in **her** room?	*Was ist in **ihrem** Zimmer?*
That's **his** computer.	*Das ist **sein** Computer.*
Who's **our** caller today?	*Wer ist heute **unser** Anrufer?*
This is **your** song.	*Dies ist **euer** Lied.*
They are in **their** house.	*Sie sind in **ihrem** Haus.*

there is, there are *(da ist, da sind)*

	There is	a dog.
	Da ist	*ein Hund.*
And	**there are**	two cats.
Und	***da sind***	*zwei Katzen.*

Cartoon: There is a dog ...

Checklist

Ich kann	
… sagen, was ich regelmäßig tue.	I go jogging on Tuesday.
… sagen, was ich immer tue.	I always play cool music.
… sagen, was ich oft tue.	I often phone my friends.
… sagen, was ich manchmal tue.	I sometimes talk about problems.
… sagen, was ich nie tue.	I never phone my teacher.
… sagen, wem etwas gehört.	That's his computer.
… anbieten, jemandem einen Gefallen zu tun.	What can I play for you?
… ein Bild beschreiben.	There are three boys with skateboards. There is a dog.
… sagen, was ich am liebsten habe.	It's my favourite song.

Checkout: A trick with numbers

Practise with a friend.

Think of a number from one to ten.

Multiply the number by two. →	x 2
Add the number eight. →	+ 8
Divide the number by two. →	÷ 2
Take away the first number. →	– first number

Your number is four.

The answer is always four.

Dies ist einer von Sams „tricks".
Probier ihn aus!
Hier gibt es wieder einige Wörter oder Wendungen, die du nicht kennst.
Du kannst sie in der alphabetischen Wortliste nachschlagen oder aus dem Zusammenhang erschließen.

TIPP

Tipps: A trick with numbers

1. Think: *Wenn ein Satz mit einem Verb beginnt, dann ist das eine Aufforderung.*
2. multiply, add, divide: *Die englischen Wörter sind so ähnlich wie im Deutschen. Zur Sicherheit kannst du dir auch die Rechenzeichen auf der rechten Seite ansehen.*

In town

1. post office
2. car park
3. café
4. market
5. next to
6. opposite
7. clock
8. What time is it?
9. four o'clock
10. ten past four
11. quarter past four
12. half past four/ four thirty
13. twenty to five
14. three fifty-two

1. *Look at the picture.* Where is it?
   The café is in … Road.
   The post office is next to the … .
2. You're in town. *Make dialogues.*
3. What time is it? *Look at the clocks.*
   Number 9: It's four o'clock.
   Number 10: It's … . *Go on, please.*

Speaking

Where's the school?

It's in London Road, opposite the post office.

Thank you.

Where's …?

Go on, please.

Let's meet at three o'clock.

OK. Where can we meet?

At the market.

Let's meet … .

Go on, please.

4. *Look at the clocks and listen.* What number is it?
   1. That's number 11.
   2. That's … . *Go on, please.*
5. Let's meet. *Make dialogues.*
6. Where's Susie?
7. What's in Tom's rucksack? What's missing?

In Greenwich

a
Greenwich is an interesting part of London. People can go to Greenwich by bus, by train and by Underground.

1

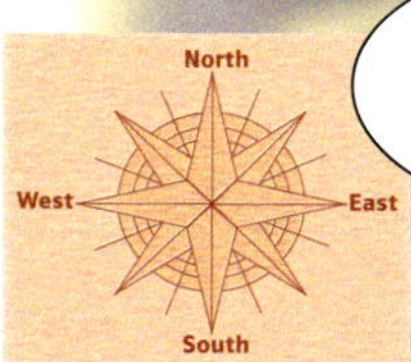

2

The Royal Observatory is in Greenwich. It's the home of the Meridian Line.

3

The Cutty Sark is a boat. It's very interesting. There's a tunnel next to the Cutty Sark. Tourists can walk under the River Thames.

Greenwich has got a famous market. Lots of people go to Greenwich Market.

1 Greenwich pictures

Sam is in Greenwich. *Match the sentences to the pictures.*

1. "The River Thames is in Greenwich."
2. "I like the old boat."
3. "Greenwich Market is very famous."
4. "Here is the Meridian Line."

That's picture … .
Go on, please.

2 An interesting part of London

Greenwich is	a famous market.
People can go to	to the market.
The Royal Observatory is	a boat.
Tourists can walk	an interesting part of London.
The Cutty Sark is	Greenwich by bus, by train and by Underground.
Greenwich has got	under the River Thames.
Lots of people go	the home of the Meridian Line.

3 Listening: A tourist in Greenwich

What's right?

1. Under the River Thames there's …
   a) a boat.
   b) a bus.
   c) a tunnel.
2. Greenwich Market is …
   a) interesting.
   b) modern.
   c) boring.
3. The tourist is …
   a) in Romney Road.
   b) under the River Thames.
   c) next to the Cutty Sark.

b Two tourists are in Greenwich. They've got a map.

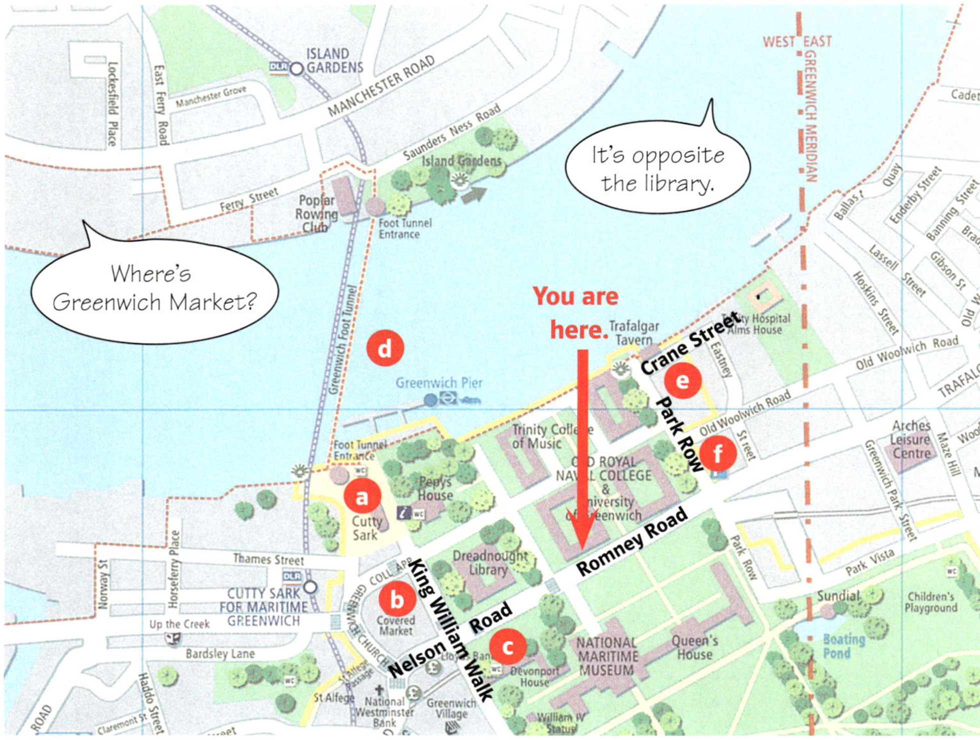

- **a** **The Cutty Sark**
- **b** **Greenwich Market**
- **c** **The Garden Restaurant**
- **d** **Tunnel under the Thames**
- **e** **Sports shop**
- **f** **Blue Note Café**

4 What is it?

1. It's in King William Walk. That's Greenwich Market.
2. It's opposite the library. That's … . *Go on, please.*
3. It's next to the tunnel.
4. It's in Crane Street.
5. It's under the Thames.

c *Man:* Excuse me. Where's the Cutty Sark?

Woman: Go along Romney Road. Turn right into King William Walk. Go straight on. The Cutty Sark is on the left. It's opposite the Information Centre.

Say it!

Go along the road.	*Geh die Straße entlang.*
Turn right.	*Geh nach rechts.*
Turn left.	*Geh nach links.*
Go straight on.	*Geh geradeaus.*

5 Speaking: Excuse me

a) *What is it? Look at the map.*

Go along Romney Road. Turn left into Park Row. Go straight on. Turn right into Crane Street. It's on the right.

b) *Make dialogues. You are in Romney Road.*

A: Excuse me. Where's the Garden Restaurant?

B: Go straight on. Go into … . It's on the … .

d *Terry:* I go to Greenwich every Saturday. I always take the train, I don't go by bus.
I sometimes meet my friends in town.
We meet at Burger Bar. We don't go there every week.
Emma goes to Greenwich every Saturday, too. She likes the market, and she goes to the shops. But she doesn't go to the sports shop.

Say it!

I **don't go** by bus.
*Ich **fahre nicht** mit dem Bus.*
She **doesn't go** to the sports shop.
*Sie **geht nicht** in das Sportgeschäft.*

6 In town

+	–
take the bus	take the Underground
buy comics	buy CDs
meet friends	meet teachers
go to the shops	go to the market

a) The friends often go to Greenwich.
Look at the list. What's missing?

Lisa: I often go to Greenwich.
I take the bus. I don't … the Underground.
Sam: I like the shops in Greenwich.
I … comics. I … CDs.
Emma: I like Burger Bar.
I … friends there.
I … teachers.
Terry: Saturday is my favourite day.
I … to the shops. I … to the market.

b) *Look at the list again.*
Then talk about the friends.

1. Lisa often goes to Greenwich.
She takes the bus. She doesn't … the Underground.
2. Sam likes the shops in Greenwich.
He … comics. He … CDs.
3. Emma likes Burger Bar.
She … friends there. She … teachers.
4. Saturday is Terry's favourite day.
He … to the shops. He … to the market.

7 Your day in town

Say what you and your friends do.
Say what you don't do.

We look at … . We don't look at … .
We go to … . We don't go to … .

e It's project day at Thomas Tallis. Every year pupils in Year 7 write a project. They work in groups. Sam, Lisa, Terry and Emma are in one group.

Sam: Do you know the questions?
Lisa: Yes, I do. They're on the worksheets.
Terry: Here's one: Why do lots of tourists come to Greenwich?
Sam: Where do we start?
Emma: Let's go to the Tourist Information Centre. We can start there.

Say it!
Do you **know** the questions? ***Weißt du** die Fragen?*
Yes, I do. *Ja.*
No, I don't. *Nein.*

8 Questions

What are the questions for the project?

a)
1. lots of tourists/come to Greenwich?
   Do lots of tourists come to Greenwich?
2. tourists/like Greenwich?
   Do …? *Go on, please.*
3. they/come by boat/or by train?
4. they/walk under the River Thames?
5. they/go to the Royal Observatory?

b)
1. what/tourists/do in Greenwich?
   What do tourists do in Greenwich?
2. how/tourists/come to Greenwich?
   How …? *Go on, please.*
3. why/they/like Greenwich?
4. where/they/start?

f It's eleven o'clock. The group is in the Tourist Information Centre. Jenny works there.

Emma: Do tourists like Greenwich?
Jenny: Yes, they do.
Emma: Do you speak German?
Jenny: No, I don't.
Sam: Do you hear the same questions every day?
Jenny: Yes, I do. And every year you come with the same project.

Say it!
Yes, they do. *Ja.*
No, they don't. *Nein.*

9 Jenny

Find Jenny's answers.

1. Do you work here? – Yes, I do.
2. Do you speak German? – *Go on, please.*
3. Do tourists like Greenwich?
4. Do pupils come with the same project every year?
5. Do you hear the same questions every day?

No, I don't.

Yes, I do.

Yes, they do.

g It's twelve thirty. The group is at the Royal Observatory.

Terry: What does GMT mean?
Lisa: Greenwich Meal Time.
Terry: Greenwich Meal Time? Are you sure? Does it mean that?
Emma: No, it doesn't. It means Greenwich Mean Time. World Time starts in Greenwich. It's twelve thirty here. It's one thirty in Germany.
Sam: Look at that!
Lisa: What is it?
Sam: It's an old clock.
Lisa: Does the clock work?
Sam: No, it doesn't.

Say it!

Does the clock **work?**	***Funktioniert*** *die Uhr?*
Yes, it does.	*Ja*
No, it doesn't.	*Nein*

10 Speaking: Questions and answers

Make dialogues with a partner.

Does
- Sam like the Royal Observatory? (+)
- the old clock work? (–)
- World Time start in New York? (–)
- GMT mean Greenwich Meal Time? (–)
- Lisa look at the clock (+)

A: Does Sam like the Royal Observatory?
B: Yes, he does.
A: *Go on, please.*

Do
- the pupils write about Greenwich? (+)
- Emma and Lisa like the project? (+)
- trains go to Greenwich? (+)
- Terry and Sam go into the tunnel? (–)
- all tourists look at the Cutty Sark? (–)

A: Do the pupils write about Greenwich?
B: Yes, they do.
A: *Go on, please.*

11 Listening: Project day

What's missing?

1. Lots of tourists come to … .
2. … works in the Tourist Information Centre.
3. Emma and Terry like … .
4. Not all tourists go into the … .

A cool idea?

Project day starts at half past nine. The teacher, Mr Rose, has got the worksheets. The pupils go to Greenwich by bus. They work in groups there.

Mr Hu: It's ten o'clock in the morning. Why are you not at school today? Is it Year 7 project day?
Sam: Yes, it is.
Mr Hu: Have you got the same questions? Every year I answer the same questions.
Lisa: When does your restaurant open? When does it close?
Mr Hu: OK, I can give you the answers … .

Terry: We've got the information about tourists, shops and restaurants. Now let's find people and ask questions.
Sam: What do we ask?
Emma: Where do you live? Do you live in Greenwich? Do you work in Greenwich?
Lisa: Oh, this is so boring! Let's go to Burger Bar.
Sam: I've got an idea. We've got the questions. We can make up the answers.
Terry: Make up the answers?
Sam: Yes.
Emma: We can't do that.
Sam: Terry, you can ask me. You can ask Lisa and Emma. We can give you the answers. Mr Rose can't find out.
Lisa: Yes, that's a cool idea.
Emma: You two are so lazy!
Sam: Not lazy, Emma, clever.

Mr Rose: Hello, boys and girls. How is your project?
Sam: It's hard. But it's OK.
Mr Rose: Good. Are your worksheets ready?
Sam: No, they aren't. Our plan is to ask people about Greenwich.
Mr Rose: Good idea. You've got time. It's two fifteen. You can talk to lots of people. We can meet at school at four o'clock.

Emma: Make up the answers. Go to Burger Bar. Good idea, Sam!
Sam: How does he know?
Terry: Mr Rose does this project every year. He knows all the tricks.

1 Project day

Answer the questions.

1. How do the pupils go to Greenwich?
2. What has Mr Rose got?
3. Who answers the same questions every year?
4. Where does Mr Rose find the friends?
5. What is hard?
6. Are the worksheets ready?
7. Who knows all the tricks?

1. They go to Greenwich by bus.
2. *Go on, please.*

2 Clocks

Find all the times in the unit. Then talk about project day.

9.30	Project day starts at half past nine.
10.00	Terry's group goes … .
11.00	
12.30	
2.00	
2.15	
4.00	

1 Where do they go?

a) *Make questions.* do does

1. Where … tourists go in Greenwich?
2. … Sam like the project?
3. Where … the friends meet?
4. … you like my picture, Lisa?
5. … Lisa know Sam's phone number?
6. When … the project start?
7. What … GMT mean?

b) *Make up the answers.*
1. They go to the Cutty Sark.
2. *Go on, please.*

2 Speaking: Yes, I do

a) *Make questions with a partner.*

Do Does	you your sister your brother your cousin your friends your parents your teachers	play football listen to the radio read comics go jogging play music meet friends play computer games go to the shops	at the weekend? on Saturday? at 9 o'clock? for the school team? after school? on Tuesday? with friends?

b) *Now answer the questions.*

A: Do you listen to the radio after school?
B: Yes, I do.

3 Project: Your town

What's interesting in your town?

Make a poster with pictures and words.

4 Project: You and your town

a) *Ask your friends. Make a list.*

Do you like your town?
Do you go into town on Saturday?
Do you take the bus?
Do you go by bike?

b) *Talk about your list in class.*

Six pupils like their town.
Three pupils don't … . *Go on, please.*

yes	no
~~IIII~~ I	III

5 When does it open?

Make sentences.

1. The Garden Restaurant opens at twelve o'clock. It closes at eleven o'clock.

2. The Blue Note Café … . *Go on, please.*

1	2	3	4	5
Garden Restaurant 12.00 – 11.00	Blue Note Café 10.30 – 5.00	Sports shop 9.30 – 6.00	Computer shop 10.00 – 7.00	Tourist Information Centre 10.00 – 5.30

6 Speaking: A day with Jenny

get up	have breakfast	go to Greenwich	have lunch	go home	meet friends	go to bed
7.00	7.30	8.00	1.00	5.30	7.30	10.00

Make questions about Jenny. Then ask a partner.

A: When does Jenny get up?
B: She gets up at seven o'clock.
A: When … ? *Go on, please.*

7 Speaking: And your friend?

Ask a friend.

A: When do you get up?
B: I get up at half past six.
A: When … ?
Go on, please.

go to school? | get up? | come home from school? | do homework? | have breakfast?

TIPP

Tipp: Wörterlernen in Sätzen und Vorstellungsbildern
Lerne ein Wort möglichst in einem ganzen Satz. Das ist für das Gedächtnis leichter.
Am besten geht es mit Sätzen, die Vorstellungsbilder in dir erzeugen, zum Beispiel wie etwas aussieht, wie es sich anhört, wie es sich anfühlt und welche Gefühle es in dir weckt.
Du kannst es am Beispiel der Reime in Übung 10 ausprobieren.

8 Word web: In town

Make a word web in your exercise book for 'in town'.

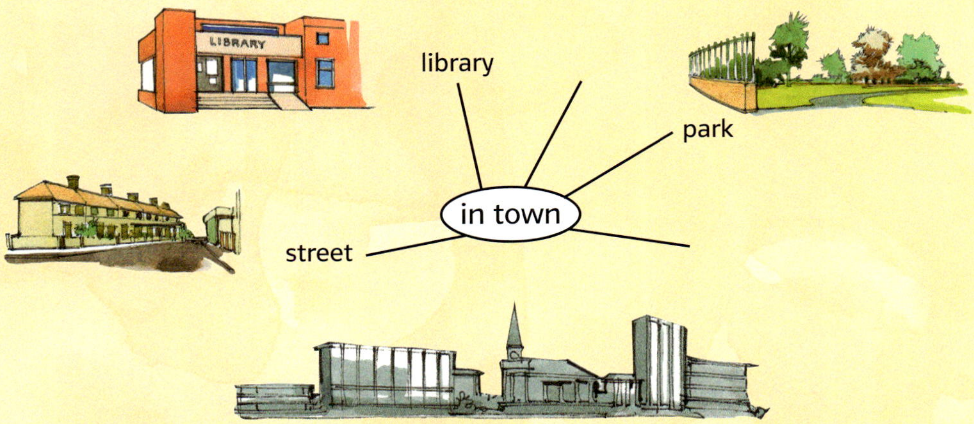

9 Signs

1

2

3

4

5
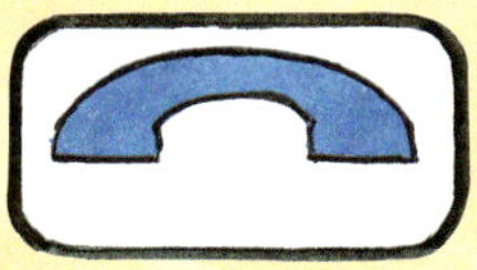

6

What's the right sign?

Picture 1: That's … .
Go on, please.

Go straight on.	Turn right.	Turn left.
The Underground	The Information Centre	A telephone

10 Listen and speak

[r]
There's a rabbit in a restaurant,
A rock star in a tree.
There's my brother on the radio,
And my grandma's here with me.

[w]
We're worried on a Wednesday,
Our worksheets aren't OK.
We go swimming at the weekend.
Why can't we play today?

11 A cartoon

caution — *Vorsicht*
meaningless — *sinnlos*

12 Picture words

Here are more picture words. Make picture words with the words 'tourist', 'tunnel' and 'turn right'.

13 Problems!

Where's Emma's mobile phone?
Match the sentences to the pictures.

in	on	under

1. Emma's mobile phone is in her bag.
2. Her mobile phone is on … .
3. It's … .
   Go on, please.

bag table chair cupboard sweatshirt TV

Present simple *(einfache Gegenwart)*

- present simple mit *I/you*

Aussage	**I go** jogging every day. **I like** the market.	***Ich gehe*** *jeden Tag joggen.* ***Ich mag*** *den Markt.*
Verneinung	**I don't go** to Greenwich. **I don't like** the market.	***Ich fahre nicht*** *nach Greenwich.* ***Ich mag*** *den Markt* ***nicht.***
Ja/Nein-Frage	**Do you** go by bike? – **Yes, I do.** – **No, I don't.**	***Fährst du*** *mit dem Fahrrad?* ***– Ja.*** ***– Nein.***
wh-Frage	Where **do you live?**	*Wo* ***wohnst du?***

- present simple mit *he/she*

Aussage	**She speaks** German. **He likes** basketball.	***Sie spricht*** *Deutsch.* ***Er mag*** *Basketball.*
Verneinung	**She doesn't** speak English. **He doesn't like** football.	***Sie spricht nicht*** *Englisch.* ***Er mag*** *Fußball* ***nicht.***
Ja/Nein-Frage	**Does she speak** English? – **Yes, she does.** – **No, she doesn't.**	***Spricht sie*** *Englisch?* ***– Ja.*** ***– Nein.***
wh-Frage	When **does he get up?**	*Wann* ***steht er auf?***

Imperative *(Befehlsform)*

Turn right. **Go** straight on.	***Geh*** *nach rechts.* ***Geh*** *geradeaus.*

Cartoon: I always go by bus.

Cartoon: Does she like football?

Checklist

Ich kann	
… jemanden freundlich ansprechen.	Excuse me.
… jemandem den Weg beschreiben.	Look left./Go straight on.
… sagen, wo etwas ist.	It's next to the market./It's opposite the shop.
… sagen, welches Verkehrsmittel ich nicht benutze.	I don't go by bus.
… fragen, ob jemand das Fahrrad benutzt.	Do you go by bike?
… auf Fragen kurze Antworten geben.	Yes, I do./No, I don't.
… fragen, ob etwas funktioniert.	Does the clock work?
… mich über etwas vergewissern.	Are you sure?
… mich nach dem Stand der Arbeit erkundigen.	How is your project?
… jemandem die Uhrzeit sagen.	It's two fifteen./It's half past nine.
… meinen Tagesablauf beschreiben.	I get up at seven o'clock.

Checkout: The fastest boat on Earth

The Cutty Sark is a very old boat.
She first sailed in 1869, and she was the fastest boat on the sea.
She took tea from China and wool from Australia to England.
Later she was a training boat for sailors. She's a museum now.
Every day you can see lots of people on her deck – tourists, not sailors.

Magst du alte Schiffe? Dann lies diesen Text und finde mehr über die Cutty Sark heraus.
Hier gibt es wieder einige Wörter oder Wendungen, die du nicht kennst.
Du kannst sie in der alphabetischen Wortliste nachschlagen oder aus dem Zusammenhang erschließen.

TIPP

Tipps: The fastest boat on Earth

1. sea, sailor, deck: *Alle Wörter sind Begriffe aus der Schifffahrt.*
2. sailed, was, took: *Diese Wörter sind Verbformen der Vergangenheit. Hier sind die Gegenwartsformen:* sails (sailed), is (was), takes (took).
3. fastest: Fastest *ist eine Form der Steigerung. Die Grundform ist* fast.

Party time!

1. robot
2. clown
3. food
4. sandwich
5. T-shirt
6. trousers
7. skirt
8. hat
9. clothes

1. A mouse, a cat, a robot and a monster are at Tom's party.
   Who's who? *Listen and find out.*
   Mark is the robot. Linda is the … . Tim … . Anna … .

2. *Make dialogues about a party.*

3. What clothes are there in the picture?
   There's a red T-shirt. There are brown trousers.
   There's … .   *Go on, please.*

Mouse rap

Let's go to a party,
you can be a frog!
I can be a robot man,
and he can be a dog!

Speaking

Let's have a party.

OK, I can be a frog.
And you?

I can be ... .

Go on, please.

What are your favourite clothes?

A pink T-shirt and green trousers.
What are your favourite clothes?

A ... .

Go on, please.

4. *Make dialogues about your favourite clothes.*
5. *Listen to the mouse rap.* Can you say it?
6. Where's Susie?
7. What's in Tom's rucksack? What's missing?

Happy birthday!

a

1st	**first**
2nd	**second**
3rd	**third**
4th	fourth
5th	fi**f**th
6th	sixth
7th	seventh
8th	eigh**th**
9th	ni**n**th
10th	tenth
11th	eleventh
12th	twel**fth**
13th	thirteenth
14th	fourteenth

15th	fifteenth
16th	sixteenth
17th	seventeenth
18th	eighteenth
19th	nineteenth
20th	twent**ieth**
21st	twenty-**first**
22nd	twenty-**second**
23rd	twenty-**third**
…	
30th	thirt**ieth**
…	
100th	hundredth
…	

1 Listening: Emma's birthday list

a) *Match the names and the dates.*

Mum → 18th January	30th September
Nasreen	3rd December
Emma	18th January
Lisa	22nd July
Sam	7th February
Terry	24th June
Dad	11th May

b) *Say the dates.*

Mrs Brook's birthday is on 18th January. *Go on, please.*

2 Speaking: Your birthday

Make dialogues with a partner.

A: When's your birthday?
B: It's on … .

A: When's your mum's birthday?
B: It's … . *Go on, please.*

3 An invitation

Make an invitation for your birthday.

b Birthdays are fun.

4 Speaking: You and your friends

a) *Make questions.*

Do	you your friends your parents	get give have like make send sing	birthdays? you cards? nice presents? a party every year? a party at home? a birthday cake? 'Happy Birthday'?

b) *Now make dialogues with a partner.*

A: Do you like birthdays?
B: Yes, I do.
A: Do your friends … a birthday cake?
B: No, they don't.

c It's Emma's birthday soon.

Emma: Can I have a party this year, Mum?
Mrs Brook: A party? Where?
Emma: Here at home.
Mrs Brook: Sorry. We're very busy, Emma. That's too much stress.
Emma: Too much stress? But I'd like a birthday cake and I'd like lots of nice presents.
Mr Brook: Anything else?

Say it!

I'**d like** a birthday cake.
*Ich **hätte gern** einen Geburtstagskuchen.*

5 Presents

What does Emma say?

1. I'd like a CD by XTM.
2. I'd like … .
Go on, please.

a CD by XTM
a cool sweatshirt
a new computer game
in-line skates
a poster of Brad Pitt
a new mobile phone

d Emma is in the kitchen with Nasreen.

Emma: Why are Mum and Dad so stressed?
Nasreen: I don't know. Would you like a sandwich?
Emma: No, thanks. I'd like a drink.
Nasreen: What would you like? Milk or orange juice?
Emma: I'd like a glass of milk, please.

Say it!

Would you **like** a sandwich?
***Möchtest** du ein Sandwich?*

6 Speaking: What would you like?

Make dialogues with a partner.

A: Would you like … ?
B: No, thanks.

A: Would you like … ?
B: Yes, please.

yes, please	no, thanks
this CD this comic this computer game …	an apple a rabbit a basketball …

e Emma's birthday is on Sunday. Terry and Sam are in a shop.

Terry: This T-shirt is nice.
Sam: Yes, the colour is very nice.
Terry: Look here. These bags are cool.
Sam: How much are they?
Terry: They're £30.
Sam: That's expensive. Let's go to the market. I'd like to look at the things there.

Say it!

This T-shirt is nice.	***Dieses T-shirt ist*** *schön.*
These bags are cool.	***Diese Taschen sind*** *cool.*
I'd like to go.	*Ich* ***möchte*** *gehen.*

7 These CDs are great

What's missing?

This | These

1. … CDs are great.
   These CDs are great.
2. … books are boring.
3. … guitar is nice.
4. … comics are awful.
5. … basketball is cool.
6. … skateboard is new.

8 Speaking: At the market

a) *Act the dialogue with a partner.*

A: Look at these CDs.
B: They're great.
A: Do you like this sweatshirt?
B: No, it's awful.

b) *Make new dialogues.*

cool
nice
new

boring
too small

basketball
guitar
T-shirt
comics
books
skateboard
skirt

f Sam's cousin Dan gets lots of e-mails.
He often says happy birthday to people.

> **Say it!**
> Can you play a song for **me**?
> *Kannst du ein Lied für **mich** spielen?*
> I like **him**. *Ich mag **ihn**.*

Hi Dan,
You're my favourite DJ. I always listen to you.
Can you play a song by Will Young for me?
I really like him!
Helen

Hello Dan,
My friend's birthday is on May 11. She's 12.
Can you say happy birthday to her?
Her name is Emma. Thanks.
Lisa

9 E-mails for Galaxy Radio

What's missing?

him	her	me	you

1. I'd like to hear 'With Time'. Can you play it for …? Please!
2. My brother is 12 tomorrow. Can you say happy birthday to … ?
3. My mother likes David Bowie. Can you play one of his CDs for …?
4. My friends love your programme, Dan. They listen to … every day.
5. My friend Jenny is a fan of Will Young. Please play his new CD for … .
6. Our sports teacher, Mr Clark, is really cool. Please play a Beatles song for … .

g Terry and his friends are at Galaxy Radio.

Terry: Dad, I'm at Galaxy Radio with Sam. Can you fetch us, please?
Mr Jackson: OK, Terry.
Terry: Lisa and Emma are also here. Can we take them, too?
Mr Jackson: Now you're four. I've got a taxi, not a bus.

> **Say it!**
> Can you fetch **us**?
> *Kannst du **uns** abholen?*
> Can we take **them**?
> *Können wir **sie** mitnehmen?*

10 In Mr Jackson's taxi

Write the sentences with 'us' or 'them'.

1. Hey, Sam. You can sit next to (Emma and me).
   Hey, Sam. You can sit next to us.
2. I can't find my CDs. Who has got (the CDs)?
   I can't … . *Go on, please.*
3. This poster is a present for (Sam and me).
4. I don't like (these sandwiches). They're awful.
5. You can give (the comics) to me.
6. Can you phone (Terry and me) in the morning?

h Mr Jackson is a taxi driver. Mrs Jackson is a journalist. Their days are very long.

6.00	get up	7.00
6.15	have breakfast	7.30
7.00	start work	9.00
12.30	have lunch	1.00
4.00	finish work	6.30
4.45	come home	7.15
7.30	have dinner	7.30
10.00	go to bed	11.00

11 A long day

a) *Look at the list. What do they say?*

Mr Jackson: I get up at six o'clock in the morning. I … . *Go on, please.*
Mrs Jackson: I get up at seven o'clock. I … . *Go on, please.*

b) *Now talk about Mr and Mrs Jackson.*

Mr Jackson gets up at … .
He … . *Go on, please.*
Mrs Jackson gets up at … .
She … . *Go on, please.*

12 Speaking: In a shop

a) *Act the dialogue with a partner.*

A: Can I help you?
B: I'd like a ruler.
A: Here you are.
B: How much is it?
A: It's £1.99.
B: OK. That's fine.
A: Would you like anything else?
B: No, thanks.

b) *Make new dialogues.*

an exercise book	£3.00
a pen for school	£4.99
a pencil case	£1.25
felt-tips	£2.50
five pencils	£1.15

Say it!
one pound fifteen
ein Pfund fünfzehn

13 Listening: Lisa goes shopping

Right or wrong?

1. Lisa would like to buy a present for a friend.
2. Lisa's friend is a boy.
3. Her friend likes girl bands.
4. The new CD by the X-Boys is £15.
5. Lisa buys the poster with a rabbit.
6. The poster is £8.
7. Lisa also buys a CD.

A special present

Emma's birthday is on Sunday. Her parents are still stressed. But Emma is happy, because she can sleep at Lisa's flat on Friday and Saturday. Emma doesn't know why her parents are so stressed.

It's Saturday. Lisa and Emma are in Lisa's flat. They are in the bedroom.

Emma: You've got a really nice room, Lisa.
Lisa: But it's small. You've got a big room in your house.
Emma: And my sister is in the room with me. She's awful. My mother is awful, too. I'd like a party this year. "It's too much stress!" she says. I'm twelve tomorrow and I can't have a party. How sad is that?
Lisa: Come on, Emma. I've got a new DVD. Would you like to see it? It's cool.
Emma: Good idea.

It's Sunday. Emma is back at home. It's her birthday.

Emma: I'm back. Hello, everybody!
Mrs Brook: Happy birthday, Emma.
Emma: Thank you.
Mrs Brook: We've got a nice present for you, Emma.
Mr Brook: It's here in the flat. You can look for it.
Emma: Look for it?
Nasreen: Yes, and we can say 'hot' or 'cold'.

Emma: Is it in the living room?
Nasreen: Cold!
Emma: OK. Is it in our room?
Mr Brook: Cold!
Emma: Which room is it? The kitchen?
Nasreen: Cold again.

Emma can't find the present. Then she looks at the door to the attic.

Mr Brook: Hot!
Emma: I can't go in that room. There are spiders in there. I hate spiders.
Nasreen: Open the door, Emma.

Emma opens the door.

Mrs Brook: Happy birthday, Emma. This is your present.
Emma: My own room!
Mr Brook: This is why we are stressed.
Emma: This is so cool. My own room and those are my favourite colours.
Nasreen: This present is from us, too. It's a special birthday cake with my design!
Emma: This is fantastic! Thank you. I'm so happy!
Nasreen: You're welcome!

1 Emma's birthday

Answer the questions.

1. Where's Emma on Saturday?
2. Why can't Emma have a birthday party?
3. When does Emma go home?
4. Where does Emma look for her present?
5. Why does she hate the attic?
6. What's Emma's first present?
7. What's her second present?
8. Why is Emma so happy now?

2 Your design

Make a design for a birthday cake.

1 At a party

a) *What's missing?*

This | These

1. … card is from Terry.
2. … CDs are so cool.
3. … games are boring.
4. … cake is nice.
5. … posters are very good.
6. … girl is a chatterbox.

b) *What's missing?*

That | Those

1. … bag on the sofa is really nice.
2. … snacks in the kitchen are awful.
3. … dog in the garden is clever.
4. … rooms next to the bathroom are tidy.
5. … card on the board is funny.
6. … presents under the table are nice.

2 Sometimes …

What's the right order? Make sentences.

1. to Greenwich/go/we/sometimes
   We sometimes go to Greenwich.
2. often/we/by bus/go
   Go on, please.
3. meet friends/we/sometimes/in the park
4. always/my mother/at the market/things/buys
5. Dad and I/look at/the sports shops/often
6. in a café/Mum and Dad/have a coffee/always

3 Project: A birthday puzzle

1

Take an old birthday card. Cut it in half.

2

Write a message on the picture half.

3

Cut the card into pieces and put them in an envelope.

4

Send your card.

cut – *schneiden*; in half – *in Hälften*; message – *Grüße, Nachricht*; piece – *Stück*; envelope – *Umschlag*

4 Can you see me in the photo?

Emma and her mother have got a photo.
What's missing?

me	you	her	us	them

Mrs Brook: Are you in the photo, Emma? I can't see … .
Emma: I'm next to Nasreen. Can you see … now?
Mrs Brook: And where's Lisa? I can't see … .
Emma: Can you see Terry and Sam?
Mrs Brook: Yes. I can see … .
Emma: Lisa is next to Terry and Sam.
Mrs Brook: Yes, I can see … now.
Emma: We're all in the photo. Why can't you see …?
Mrs Brook: It isn't a good photo and I haven't got my glasses.

5 Speaking: What can we do?

a) *Act the dialogue with a partner.*

A: Hi. What can we do?
B: Let's go to the cinema.
A: Good idea. I'd like to see 'Mr Bean in India'.
B: We can phone Mark. I'm sure he'd like to come with us.
A: We can go at two o'clock.
B: OK. We can meet outside the cinema.

b) *Make new dialogues.*

What film?
Say the name of your favourite film.

When?
Say when you can meet.

Who?
Say a friend's name.

Where?
Say where you can meet.

6 Speaking: When can we meet?

Ben and Nasreen would like to meet.

a) *Act the dialogue.*

Nasreen: Let's meet on 3rd January.
Ben: I'm sorry. I've got a party that evening.
Nasreen: And the eighth?
Ben: Oh no, that's my sister's sixth birthday.
Nasreen: The tenth, then?
Ben: That's OK.

b) *Make new dialogues.*

Find new dates.

a football game
a school project
a basketball game
…

my mother, 40
my cousin, 21
my brother, 18

> **TIPP**
>
> **Tipp: Wörterlernen durch Wortbeziehungen**
>
> Suche bereits vorhandene Wörter, an denen du die neuen Wörter festmachen kannst. Dazu gibt es verschiedene Tricks, wie du dein Gedächtnis überlisten kannst.
> Beispiele findest du in den Übungen 9 (Reim: crazy – lazy), 13 (Gegensatz: hot – cold) und 11 (Sachfeld: week – Thursday).

7 Word web: Birthdays

Make a word web in your exercise book for 'birthdays'.

8 Fun questions

a) What does the birthday cake say to the ice cream?

b) What is it?
You can find one in June.
You can find one in July.
And you can find two in August.

a) You're so cool!   b) The letter u.

9 Listen and speak

[θ]

Thirty thirsty people are coming
here on Thursday.
Thirty thirsty people, you see, it is
my birthday.

Thirty thirsty people,
their things are fun and crazy.
Thirteen of them are clever
and three of them are lazy!

10 Which word is it?

| when | what |
| which | who |

a) *Make the questions.*

1. … does Nasreen give Emma?
2. … room does Emma get?
3. … does Emma sleep at Lisa's house?
4. … group does Emma like?
5. …'d like to have a party in the park?

b) *Find the answers. They are in the unit.*

11 What's missing?

1. first, …, third, fourth
2. …, April, May, June
3. seventh, …, ninth, tenth
4. Tuesday, …, Thursday, Friday
5. November, December, January, …
6. eleventh, …, thirteenth, fourteenth

12 One word is wrong!

1. green, cold, yellow, brown
2. tree, spider, frog, bird
3. cake, card, present, attic
4. cousin, brother, teacher, sister
5. train, bus, bridge, car
6. kitchen, cafeteria, bathroom, bedroom

13 Word pairs

Make pairs with the words.

1. look for – find
2. hot –
   Go on, please.

look for like happy
boring cold find
never always get up hot
sad go to bed hate interesting

14 Picture words

Here are more picture words. Make picture words with the words 'glasses', 'hat' and 'present'.

15 What are they?

1. the Thames – That's a river.
2. Thursday – … . *Go on, please.*
3. milk –
4. London –
5. y –
6. seventeen –
7. hockey –
8. pink –

I'd like *(ich möchte)*

Aussage	**I'd like** a party. **I'd like** a birthday cake. **I'd like to play** football. **I'd like to sing** in a band.	***Ich möchte gerne*** *eine Party.* ***Ich möchte gerne*** *einen Geburtstagskuchen.* ***Ich möchte gerne*** *Fußball* ***spielen.*** ***Ich möchte gerne*** *in einer Band* ***singen.***
Ja/Nein-Frage	**Would you like** a sandwich? – **Yes, please.** – **No, thank you.**	***Möchtest du*** *ein Sandwich?* ***– Ja, bitte.*** ***– Nein, danke.***
wh-Frage	**What would you like?**	***Was möchtest du gern?***

Personal pronouns *(Fürwörter)*

This is a song for **me**.	*Dies ist ein Lied für* ***mich****.*
This is a song for **you**.	*Dies ist ein Lied für* ***dich****.*
Can you play a song for **her**?	*Kannst du ein Lied für* ***sie*** *spielen?*
Can you play a song for **him**?	*Kannst du ein Lied für* ***ihn*** *spielen?*
Can you play a song for **us**?	*Kannst du ein Lied für* ***uns*** *spielen?*
Let's play a song for **them**.	*Lasst uns ein Lied für* ***sie*** *spielen.*

this, these *(dies, diese)*

I'd like **this** bag.	*Ich möchte* ***diese*** *Tasche.*
This bag is nice.	***Diese*** *Tasche ist hübsch.*
I'd like **these** bags.	*Ich möchte* ***diese*** *Taschen.*
These bags are nice.	***Diese*** *Taschen sind hübsch.*

Cartoon: Would you like a sandwich?

Cartoon: This bag is nice.

Checklist

Ich kann	
… genaue Angaben zur Zeit und zum Datum machen.	The party is on 5th May at 4 o'clock.
… sagen, was ich gern hätte.	I'd like an exercise book, please.
… fragen, was jemand haben möchte.	Would you like an orange juice?
… ein Angebot annehmen oder ablehnen.	Yes, please./No, thanks.
… Gegenstände genauer beschreiben.	This colour is nice./These bags are cool.
… sagen, was ich gern tun würde.	I'd like to meet a famous rock star.
… sagen, für wen etwas ist.	Can you play a song for me?
… Tagesabläufe beschreiben.	Mr Jackson comes home at 4.45.
… nach dem Preis fragen.	How much is it?
… mich mit Freunden verabreden.	Let's meet outside the cinema.

U1 Meine Person
U2 Meine Familie
U3 Meine Hobbies
U4 Mein Wohnort
U5 Mein Tagesablauf
U6 Meine Ferien
U7 Mein Schuljahr

Checkout: Seven people

Seven people went to a hotel.
They wanted to have seven rooms.
The hotel only had six rooms,
but the manager wanted to help.
He put the first person in the first room.
He asked the second person to wait.
He put the third person in the second room.
The fourth person went into the third room.
The fifth person got the fourth room.
He then put the sixth person in the fifth room.
He went to the seventh person
and gave this person the sixth room.
Was everybody happy then?

Lies den Text und beantworte die Frage am Schluss. Erkläre auf Englisch, warum jeder Hotelgast nun zufrieden oder nicht zufrieden ist.

Hier gibt es wieder einige Wörter oder Wendungen, die du nicht kennst. Du kannst sie in der alphabetischen Wortliste nachschlagen oder aus dem Zusammenhang erschließen.

TIPP

Tipps: Seven people

1. went, wanted, had, put, asked, got, was: *Alle Verbformen sind in der Vergangenheit. Die Gegenwartsformen der verwendeten Verben sind* go, want, have, put, ask, get, give, is.
2. The second person didn't get a room. *Dieser Satz steht nicht im Text, er hilft dir aber die Frage zum Text zu beantworten.*
3. didn't get *ist die Vergangenheitsform von* doesn't get.

On the farm

1. farm
2. tractor
3. river
4. pond
5. field
6. duck
7. pony
8. hen
9. sheep
10. cow
11. weather
12. rainy
13. cloudy
14. sunny

1. Tom is on the farm. He can do lots of things there.
   He can look at … . He can play with … . *Go on, please.*
2. *Talk about the weather on the farm.*
   On Monday it's … . *Go on, please.*
3. *Make dialogues about the farm.*

Speaking

What would you like to do?

I'd like to look at the cows.

OK, let's do that./ No, that's boring.

Go on, please.

Today it's rainy. What can we do?

We can watch TV.

OK, but let's … first.

Go on, please.

4. *Listen to the dialogues.* What day is it? What's the weather?
   Dialogue 1 is … . *Go on, please.*
5. *Make dialogues about the weather.*
   go outside play football go to town play at home
   do my homework watch TV work in the house
6. Where's Susie?
7. What's in Tom's rucksack? What's missing?

A holiday in Devon

a Terry's family would like to visit Devon, in southwest England. Mr Jackson has got information about Devon. The Jacksons are talking about the holiday.

Mr Jackson: I want to stay on a farm. Farms are interesting.

Terry: These activity centres are cool, too. They've got lots of things. Can we go to one of them?

Mrs Jackson: I'd like to go to the beach. There are fantastic beaches in Devon.

Mr Jackson: We can also visit Dartmoor. There are wild ponies.

Terry: Can a friend come with me? I don't want to go alone. I think that's boring.

Say it!

I **want to visit** Devon.
*Ich **will** Devon **besuchen.***
I **don't want to go** alone.
*Ich **will nicht** alleine **fahren.***

1 Holiday ideas

Match the parts of the sentences.

1. The Jacksons want to → visit Devon.
2. Mr Jackson has got
3. Mr Jackson would like to
4. Terry can do lots of things
5. Mrs Jackson would like to
6. There are wild ponies
7. Terry thinks a holiday alone

information about Devon.
visit Devon.
in an activity centre.
stay on a farm.
is boring.
go to the beach.
on Dartmoor.

2 Speaking: A holiday

a) *Look at pictures 1-4. Ask your partner.*

A: Where do you want to go?
B: I want to go to Riverford Farm.
I find farms interesting.
Where do you want to go?
A: I want to … . *Go on, please.*

b) *Make new dialogues.*

Do you want to …?

I find … boring.

No, I don't.

I don't like … .

I want to … .

3 Listening: What do you think?

Are these sentences right or wrong?

1. The Jacksons want to stay in a hotel.
   That's wrong. The Jacksons want to stay on a farm.
2. Terry thinks it's a good idea.
3. Terry would like to go with a friend.
4. Terry would like to go with Emma.
5. Terry can't phone Sam and ask him.
6. Mr and Mrs Jackson can talk to Sam's father on Sunday.

b The Jacksons are at Greendale Farm in Devon. Sam is with them. Families can stay on the farm, but they must be careful.

Sam: This is cool!
Mr Jackson: Greendale is a modern farm. You must be careful where you go, and tell us what you do. Don't feed the animals, and don't do crazy things. Farms can be dangerous!
Terry: OK, Dad.
Mr Jackson: And don't leave the farm alone.

Say it!

They **must** be careful. *Sie **müssen** vorsichtig sein.*
Don't do that. ***Mach/macht** das **nicht.***

4 Mr Jackson's rules

What does Mr Jackson say?

Don't go swimming | Don't leave | You must come back | Don't take | You must tell us | Don't feed

1. … where you are.
   You must tell us where you are.
2. … the farm alone.
   Go on, please.
3. … in the river.
4. … the animals.
5. … your bikes into the fields.
6. … to your room at six o'clock.

5 Speaking: Don't do that!

Look at the pictures. Then make dialogues with a partner.

play

go swimming

feed

sit

1. *A:* Don't play on the tractor.
   That's dangerous!
   B: I'm sorry!
   A: That's OK.
2. *A:* Don't … . *Go on, please.*

c

Sam and Terry are in their room on the farm.
Terry: What's that noise?

Sam: Mrs Richards is on the tractor. She's going to the fields.

I can see a woman. She's feeding the ducks. They're eating lots of food.

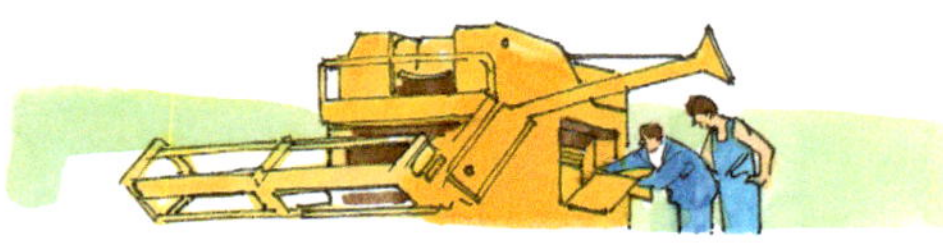

Two men are working, too. They're repairing a farm machine.

Oh, and there's Mr Richards. He's running. The bull is behind him!

Say it!
She**'s feeding** the ducks.
*Sie **füttert** gerade die Enten.*
They**'re repairing** a machine.
*Sie **reparieren** gerade eine Maschine.*

6 On the farm

Make sentences.

Mrs Richards A woman The ducks Two men They Mr Richards	is are	going to the fields. feeding the ducks. eating lots of food. working. repairing a farm machine. running.

7 Speaking: I know what you're doing!

One pupil must act.
Say what the pupil is doing.

A: I know what you're doing.
You're dancing.
B: I'm sorry. You're wrong.
A: You're playing the drums.
B: That's right.
I'm playing the drums.
Go on, please.

play the drums make a cake do a card trick
eat an apple talk on a mobile phone ...

d It's ten o'clock. Terry is talking to Emma on his mobile phone.

Emma: I hope you're working hard.
Terry: We're working very hard. We're helping on the farm. Sam is feeding the animals. Can you hear them?
Emma: I can hear music and computer games. So you aren't helping on the farm, and Sam isn't feeding the animals. You're listening to music and you're playing computer games.

Say it!
Sam **isn't feeding** the animals.
*Sam **füttert** gerade die Tiere **nicht**.*
Sam and Terry **aren't working**.
*Sam und Terry **arbeiten** gerade **nicht**.*

8 I'm sorry, that's wrong!

What's missing?

isn't | aren't

1. Mr Richards is feeding the hens. He isn't feeding the sheep.
2. Two cows are eating in a field. They aren't … . *Go on, please.*
3. Terry is sitting under a tree. He … .
4. Sam is playing with a cat. He … .
5. Two girls are working in the farm shop. They … .
6. Mrs Jackson is watching TV. She … .
7. Mr Jackson is sleeping. He … .
8. Two families are looking at the farm. They … .

+	–
feed the hens	feed the sheep
eat in a field	eat in a road
sit under a tree	sit in a tree
play with a cat	play with a dog
work in the farm shop	work in the kitchen
watch TV	listen to a CD
sleep	help Mr Richards
look at the farm	stay on the farm

9 Speaking: I hope you're working!

a) *Act the phone dialogue with a partner.*

A: I hope you're working!
B: I'm sorry. I'm not working.
I'm watching television.
A: Oh! You're awful!

b) *Make new phone dialogues.*

working helping Dad feeding the cat eating lots of vegetables	watching television reading comics playing with the cat eating lots of hamburgers

10 The Jacksons on the farm

1

2

Work with a partner. Talk about the two pictures.

1. In picture 1 Sam and Terry are playing football.
   In picture 2 they aren't playing football.
   They're playing basketball.
2. In picture 1 Mr Jackson is … . *Go on, please.*

e Sam and Terry want to sleep in their tent in a field. They've got lots of things. Terry's parents aren't happy with the plan.

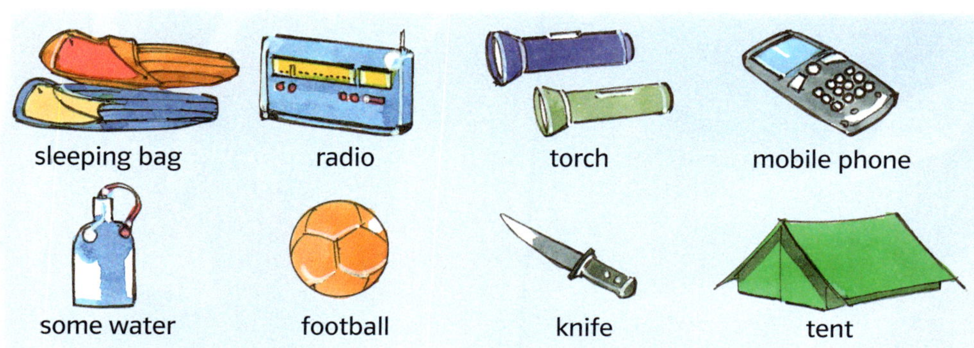

11 Have they got it?

1. Sam and Terry have got two sleeping bags.
2. They've got … .
   Go on, please.

12 Speaking: In the tent

Make dialogues with a partner.

A: Have you got the mobile phone?
B: Yes, I have. Here you are.
A: Have you got the … . *Go on, please.*

mobile phone	water
torch	radio
sleeping bag	…

13 Listening: Here are your things

1. Where are Terry and Sam?
2. What has Sam got?
3. When's breakfast?

An adventure on the farm

1

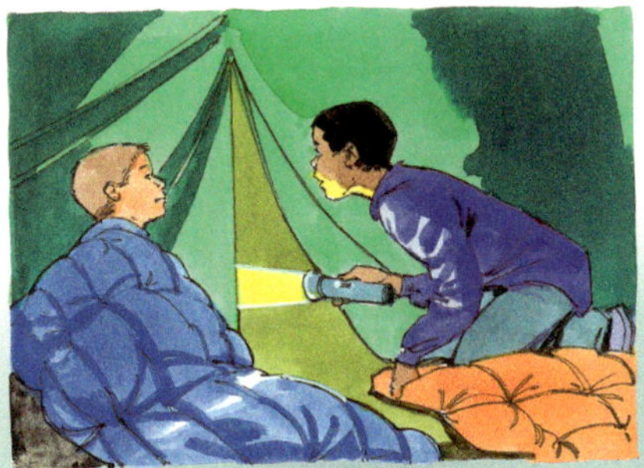

It's ten o'clock. Terry and Sam are in the tent. But they aren't sleeping.

Terry: Hey, Sam. Are you tired?
Sam: No, I'm not.
Terry: Let's go outside. There's a path next to the field. We can walk along it.
Sam: We can't leave the farm.
Terry: We've got a torch. I can find the tent again.

Terry and Sam are now walking along the path. They can see a car park. A car is in the car park. The two boys are behind a tree.

2

Sam: What can you see?
Terry: Two men are carrying a large box. They're putting it in the bushes.
Sam: Can they hear us?
Terry: No. They're going to their car now. They're driving away.
Sam: What's the number of the car?
Terry: FA 03 EDF.

3

The two boys are now looking at the box. Terry is opening it.

Sam: What's in it?
Terry: A computer. A DVD player. CDs. And a video camera. Do you think the men are criminals?
Sam: Close the box. A car is coming. They're coming back.
Terry: Let's go.

The boys are now running to their tent.

Sam: I think they're following us.

At eleven o'clock Mr and Mrs Jackson go to the tent. The boys aren't there. Terry's parents are really worried so they call the police. Now it's 11.15 and a police officer is with them. Now the boys are here, too.

Mr Jackson: Why aren't you in your tent?
Terry: I'm sorry, Dad …
Police officer: It's OK, Mr Jackson. Don't be angry. Oh, excuse me. That's my phone. We've got a break-in. I must go now.
Terry: A break-in? There's a box in the bushes near the car park. It's got a computer, a video camera, and a DVD player.
Police officer: Can you show me?
Terry: Yes. The car park is near here.
Sam: The men have got a car. The number of the car is FA 03 EDF.
Mr Jackson: OK. You can go with the police officer. But you can't sleep alone in the tent again.

4

1 The pictures

Match the parts of the sentences.

1. In picture 1 the boys → are in the tent.	are putting a box in the bushes.
2. They	are in the box.
3. In picture 2 the men	is listening to the boys.
4. Sam and Terry	is angry.
5. In picture 3 the boys	are watching them.
6. Lots of things	are in the tent.
7. In picture 4 Mr Jackson	are opening the box.
8. The police officer	aren't tired.

2 What are the words?

1. Number 1 is a path.
2. Number 2 is … .

Go on, please.

1 Crazy rules

Make crazy rules for the farm.

Don't	go swimming	with the hens.
	write e-mails	in the tractor.
	play football	on the cows.
	put eggs	in the river.
	have breakfast	with the sheep.
	put your tent	in the car park.
	…	… .

2 Farm cartoons

a) *Find the right sentences for the cartoons.*

Cartoon 1: The mother pig is feeding the young pigs. They're … . *Go on, please.*

b) *Do you like the cartoons? Say why.*

They're working with computers.
The mother pig is feeding the young pigs.
The cows have got their own room.
They're watching TV, too.
It's a very modern farm.
They're very small.

3 Project: Holiday photos

Find two or three photos from a holiday. Make a poster and write what you are doing in the photos.

In this photo my sister is with a friend.
They're wearing hats.

Here you can see me.
I'm washing a nice dog.

4 I'm sorry

1. Let's go to the river. (I/go home now)
   I'm sorry, I'm going home now.
2. Can you boys help me with these hens? (we/help Mr Jackson now)
   I'm sorry, we're … . *Go on, please.*
3. Can Mrs Richards help us with our tent? (she/feed the hens now)
4. Is Mr Richards there? (he/drive the tractor now)
5. Let's look at some photos. (I/listen to my new CD now)
6. Sam, can we play football? (I/write an e-mail now)
7. Can I talk to Mrs Jackson, please? (she/have her breakfast now)
8. Can I look at the cows with you? (I/take eggs to the market now)

5 Speaking: Matchstick people

a) *Let's draw matchstick people.*

b) *Now make dialogues with a partner.*

A: What have you got?
B: I've got a matchstick man. His name is Tom. He's sleeping now. What have you got?
A: I've got a matchstick woman. Her name is … .
Go on, please.

6 Speaking: Let's go to an activity centre

Act the dialogue with a partner.

You	Your partner
Schlage vor, an den Strand zu gehen.	*Sage, dass das langweilig ist.*
Frage, was dein Partner gerne tun würde.	*Sage, dass du gerne in einen Erlebnispark gehen würdest.*
Stimme zu und sage, dass du einen Erlebnispark cool findest.	*Schlage vor, zu gehen.*

Let's go … .

That's … .

What would you … ?

I'd like to … .

OK. An activity centre … .

Let's … .

TIPP

Tipp: Wörterlernen mit einem Partner
So geht es viel leichter! Probiert es einmal aus. Sprecht einen Dialog und benutzt ein neues Wort dabei:

A: Can I have an ice cream?
B: Yes. Here you are.

Oder probiert mit einem Partner, ein Wort durch Lippenlesen und Buchstabieren (vorwärts und rückwärts) zu üben:
h-o-l-i-d-a-y   y-a-d-i-l-o-h.
Versucht das mit den Wörtern auf dieser Seite.

7 Word web: On the farm

Make a word web in your exercise book for 'on the farm'.

8 Listen and speak

[v]	[w]
Eva drives a very nice van with very nice vegetables. She visits the farm every evening.	We're watching wild ponies. Where do they find the water when the weather is hot?

9 One word is wrong

1. cow, sheep, egg, dog
   'Egg' is wrong.
2. train, tent, knife, sleeping bag *Go on, please.*
3. tractor, pony, van, car
4. farm, book, activity centre, beach
5. walk, run, go jogging, go swimming
6. house, library, shop, duck

10 Two, three, four

What's in the pictures?

knife/knives	man/men
box/boxes	woman/women
sheep/sheep	pony/ponies

1. There are two boxes under the chair.
2. There are three … .
   Go on, please.

under the chair

in the field

on the table

in the garden

behind the door

in the car

11 Picture words

Here are more picture words. Make picture words with the words 'tent', 'path' and 'behind'.

12 Time for a song

1. Old MacDonald had a farm,
   E–I–E–I–O.
   And on his farm he had some chicks,
   E–I–E–I–O.
   With a chick-chick here,
   and a chick-chick there,
   here a chick, there a chick,
   everywhere a chick-chick.
2. … some ducks (quack-quack)
3. … some sheep (baa-baa)
4. … a pig (oink-oink)
5. … a cow (moo-moo)

had – *hatte*; chick – *Küken*; everywhere – *überall*

Present progressive *(Verlaufsform in der Gegenwart)*

- present progressive mit *I*

Aussage	**I'm working** hard. **I'm helping** on the farm.	***Ich arbeite im Moment*** *viel.* ***Ich helfe gerade*** *auf dem Bauernhof.*
Verneinung	**I'm not watching** TV.	***Ich schaue gerade nicht*** *fern.*
	I'm not doing my homework.	***Ich mache gerade nicht*** *meine Hausaufgaben.*

- present progressive mit *he, she*

Aussage	**She's listening** to the radio.	***Sie hört gerade*** *Radio.*
Verneinung	**He isn't making** a poster.	***Er macht gerade kein*** *Poster.*

Achtung: make → making; sit → sitting

want to *(wollen)*

Aussage	**I want to** visit Devon.	***Ich will*** *Devon besuchen.*
Verneinung	**I don't want to** go alone.	***Ich will nicht*** *allein fahren.*

Negative imperatives *(verneinte Befehlsform)*

Don't play on the tractor.	***Spiel/Spielt nicht*** *auf dem Traktor.*
Don't do crazy things.	***Mach/Macht keine*** *verrückten Sachen.*

Cartoon: I'm helping on the farm.

Cartoon: Don't play on the tractor!

Checklist

Ich kann	
… sagen, dass ich etwas tun will.	I want to stay on a farm.
… jemanden zur Vorsicht ermahnen.	Be careful!
… sagen, dass ich etwas nicht tun will.	I don't want to go to the beach.
… jemandem sagen, dass er etwas nicht tun soll.	Don't go swimming in the river!
… sagen, was ich gerade tue.	I'm helping the farmer.
… sagen, was ich gerade nicht tue.	I'm not watching television.
… sagen, was jemand anders gerade tut.	She's feeding the hens.
… sagen, was in einem Bild geschieht.	The men are driving away.
… sagen, dass ich jemanden schrecklich finde.	You're awful!

U1 Meine Person
U2 Meine Familie
U3 Meine Hobbies
U4 Mein Wohnort
U5 Mein Tagesablauf
U6 Meine Ferien
U7 Mein Schuljahr

Checkout: Sherlock Holmes and Doctor Watson

Sherlock Holmes and Doctor Watson are on a camping trip. It's night. They are going to bed and looking up at the sky.

Holmes: Watson, look up. What do you see?
Watson: I see thousands of stars.
Holmes: And what does that mean to you?
Watson: It means we will have a nice day tomorrow. What does it mean to you, Holmes?
Holmes: To me it means somebody has stolen our tent!

Einige von euch haben sicher schon von Sherlock Holmes und Doctor Watson gehört. Was wisst ihr über sie? Wofür ist Sherlock Holmes bekannt? Hier gibt es wieder einige Wörter oder Wendungen, die du nicht kennst. Du kannst sie in der alphabetischen Wortliste nachschlagen oder aus dem Zusammenhang erschließen.

TIPP

Tipps: Sherlock Holmes and Doctor Watson

1. will have: *Dies ist eine Verbform der Zukunft.*
2. tomorrow: *Das Wort* tomorrow *sagt, dass etwas am nächsten Tag geschehen wird.*
3. has stolen: *Diese Verbform der Vergangenheit ist im Deutschen und im Englischen sehr ähnlich.*

The school year

a

There are lots of different events in the school year at Thomas Tallis.

Autumn term

1 Year 7 disco

2 Thames Festival Lantern Procession

"We make lanterns in September. The procession is cool!"

Spring term

"Some pupils act in the school play. This year's 'play is 'Bugsy Malone'."

3 School play

4 School exchange

Exchange visit to Berlin

All Year 9 pupils who are taking part in the Berlin exchange please come to the Art room at 12.30.
Mr Rose

Summer term

"There are always funny games at the summer fair. Pupils buy and sell things, too."

1 The year at Thomas Tallis

Match the pictures with the sentences.

1. Pupils do different sports.
   That's picture number 5.
2. Pupils act in a play for parents, teachers and other pupils.
   That's ... . *Go on, please.*
3. Pupils from Years 7 and 8 make lanterns and walk along the Thames.
4. You can meet new friends, dance and listen to cool music.
5. In spring pupils from the partner school come to Thomas Tallis.
6. There are lots of different activities. Pupils sell things, too.

2 Listening: Who can help?

Right or wrong?

1. Mrs Carter is looking for people now.
   That's right.
2. The play isn't fun.
   That's ... . *Go on, please.*
3. Emma wants to be in the play.
4. Terry and the band can play the music.
5. Sam can act, too.
6. He can make a design for the play.
7. They can start on Tuesday.

3 Speaking: Your school year

Talk about your school year with a partner.
What do you do in autumn, winter, spring and summer?
Ask your teacher for new words.

- school play
- procession
- sports day
- disco
- ...

A: I like the summer. There's the summer fair. That's fun.
What do you like?
B: I like the winter ... . *Go on, please.*

1 throw the discus 2 do the long jump 3 run in a race 4 play cricket 5 take the times 6 drink water

b It's sports day at Thomas Tallis. The pupils are on the sports field. They're doing different sports. The teachers are helping. A reporter from Galaxy Radio is watching.

4 A sports reporter

a) *What does the reporter say?*

I'm at the Thomas Tallis sports day. I'm on the sports field. Some boys are playing cricket. A girl is … . Two girls are … . *Go on, please.*

b) *Not all the pupils are doing sports. Say what they're doing.*

Some of the pupils are watching. A boy and a girl are … . Some pupils are … . *Go on, please.*

c Mrs Carter is looking for Terry, Emma and Lisa.

Mrs Carter: Where's Terry?
Sam: He's on the sports field.
Mrs Carter: I can't see him. Is he throwing the discus?
Sam: Yes, he is.
Mrs Carter: And where are Lisa and Emma? What are they doing?
Sam: I think Lisa is doing the long jump.
Mrs Carter: And what are you doing?
Sam: I'm drinking some water. We've got a race at two o'clock.

Say it!

Is he throwing the discus?
Ist er gerade beim Diskuswerfen?
Are they doing the long jump?
Sind sie gerade beim Weitsprung?
What **are they doing**?
*Was **machen sie** gerade?*

5 Yes, she is!

Look at the big picture again. Find the right short answer.

1. Is Lisa doing the long jump? – Yes, she is.
2. Is Terry running in the race? – … . *Go on, please.*
3. Is the reporter watching?
4. Is Emma playing football?
5. Are the teachers playing cricket?
6. Are the teachers taking the times?
7. Is Sam drinking water?

Yes, he is.

No, he isn't.

Yes, she is.

No, she isn't.

Yes, they are.

No, they aren't.

6 Speaking: Tom's sports day

do the long jump/eat toast

play basketball/buy cornflakes

play cricket/drink milk

play tennis/make coffee

run in a race/run from the cat

sleep/eat cheese

Make dialogues with a partner.

A: Is Tom eating toast?
B: No, he isn't. He's doing the long jump.
A: Is Susie …? *Go on, please.*

7 Speaking: Sports pictures

Find pictures where people are doing sports.
Make dialogues with a partner.

A: Have you got a man or woman?
B: I've got a man.
A: What's he doing?
B: He's playing volleyball. Look!
Go on, please.

play volleyball/football/hockey/golf
run in a race do the long jump
do inline skating throw the discus

d Every year the school has a summer fair. It's usually on the sports field. Pupils and parents bring things and sell them. The money goes to the school to buy things. There are always lots of interesting stalls.

Try face painting.
Sit in a fire engine.
Play a game and win a prize.
Eat fresh hamburgers.
Listen to the school band.
Look at all the stalls.
Throw a sponge at your friends – or a teacher!

cake	£1
video	50p
game	£1.50
book	50p
CD	£2
jigsaw puzzle	90p
pencil case	75p
comic	10p

8 What can they do?

Say what pupils can do at the summer fair.

1. What can pupils listen to at the summer fair?
   They can listen to the school band.
2. Where can they sit?
   They can sit … . *Go on, please.*
3. What can they throw?
4. What other things can they do?
5. How much are the CDs?
6. How much are the comics?
7. What other things can they buy?

9 Speaking: I'd like to try it!

a) *Act the dialogue with a partner.*

A: What would you like to do?
B: I'd like to try face painting.
A: I don't want to do that. I want to listen to the school band.
B: OK. Let's do that.

b) *Make new dialogues with the activities on the board.*

Say it!
What would you like to do?
***Was würdest du gerne** tun?*

10 Here's Mr Rose!

What's missing?

Emma: I think my dad is at the fair, but I can't see … .
Lisa: My sister Jade would like a jigsaw puzzle. I must find one for … .
Terry: I like those CDs but I can't buy … . They're too expensive!
Sam: Oh, no! Here's Mr Rose. He wants to talk to … .
Mr Rose: Hello, everybody! Lisa and Emma, Mrs Carter is looking for … . And Sam and Terry, you can help … at our face painting stall. Let's go!

him | her | you
me | them | us

11 After the summer fair

The pupils can't find their things.
Match the sentences with the pictures.

1. *Simon:* Where's Peter? I've got his shoes.
2. *Terry and Sam:* Is this … ?

Where's Tara? This is her bag. | Where's Peter? I've got his shoes. | This is my sweatshirt.

Is this our book? | Tell Tom and Luke. I've got their CDs. | Is this your mobile phone?

12 Listening: Let's have a disco!

What's the right answer?

1. The pupils want to have a disco …
   a) at the end of the summer term.
   b) at the end of the autumn term.
   c) at the end of the spring term.

2. Pupils from other schools …
   a) can come to the disco.
   b) can't come to the disco.
   c) don't want to come to the disco.

3. The school has got …
   a) a disco room.
   b) a DJ.
   c) a rock band.

4. Terry is in the school band. He …
   a) dances.
   b) sings.
   c) plays the drums.

13 Speaking: The summer disco

Two pupils are talking about a poster for the summer disco.
Make dialogues with a partner.

A: When's the disco?
B: It's on Friday 15th July.
A: When … ? *Go on, please.*

When's the disco?
When does it start?
Where's the disco?
Who's the DJ?
How much are the tickets?
Who can come?

Trouble at the disco

It's 8 o'clock on Friday. The pupils from Year 7 are at the summer disco. The disco is in the school. Only pupils from Year 7 can go to the disco. Galaxy Dan is the DJ. Mr Penford, the sports teacher, is standing in front of the door.

The pupils are in two groups. The boys are in one group. The girls are in one group. They're listening to the music and they're talking.

Mrs Carter: Why aren't you dancing? You've got a disco and now you're standing in groups.

Emma: We see the boys every day in school.

Lisa: Why can't we have boys from different schools?

Mrs Carter: We don't want trouble.

Terry: Hey, Sam. You like Tara. Go and dance with her.

Sam: Leave me alone.

A window is open in the school. Two boys are climbing in. They want to go to the disco. But they aren't from Thomas Tallis.

Now the two boys are dancing with Tara and her friend. Sam and Terry are watching. They don't know who the boys are.

Sam: Who's dancing with Tara?
Terry: I don't know. Do you want to dance with her? You must be quick. You can't wait all evening.
Sam: Are they in Year 7?
Terry: I don't think they're from our school. Let's ask them.

The new boys are now arguing with a group of pupils.

Boy: What's your problem? I'm her boyfriend. Go and play with your lego.
Lisa: Where's Mr Penford? Can you find him, Emma?

Now the boys are fighting. Mr Penford is coming.

Mr Penford: What's happening?
Sam: They're not from our school, sir.
Terry: A window is open in the toilets.
Mr Penford: This disco is only for pupils from Year 7 at Thomas Tallis. Can you leave now or must I help you?
Boy: We don't want to stay. This is a boring disco. It's only for children. Come on, Matt. Let's go.
Terry: Hey, Sam, now you can dance with Tara.

1 Trouble!

1. Who can go to the disco?
2. Where is Mr Penford standing?
3. What are the boys and girls doing?
4. Why are Lisa and Emma not very happy?
5. What would Sam like to do?
6. Are the two boys from Thomas Tallis?
7. Who is dancing with the boy?
8. Why is the disco 'boring'?

1 Some days are different!

Mr Penford

Nasreen and Emma

Katie

Terry

Lisa and her friends

Mr Jackson

the girls

1. Is Mr Penford teaching sports?
   No, he isn't. He's teaching German.
2. Are Nasreen and Emma going to school by bus?
   No, … . *Go on, please.*
3. … going swimming? … .
4. … playing basketball? … .
5. … singing karaoke? … .
6. … staying at home? … .
7. … listening to music? … .

2 Speaking: Phone dialogues

Make phone dialogues with a partner.

A: Are you watching the football game?
B: No, I'm not. I'm watching the tennis game. Are you …?
Go on, please.

do	watch	drink	eat	…

3 Project: A poster for a summer fair

Make a poster in English for your school's summer fair.

The information about the Thomas Tallis summer fair can help you.
It's on page 110.

4 Speaking: Who's first?

The results for the long jump are on the board.

Talk about the results with a partner.

A: Who's first?
B: Tom Harvey.
And who's second?
A: … . *Go on, please.*

Long jump

Andy Bray	– 4.26 metres
Sam Brown	– 3.83 metres
Steven Clark	– 3.77 metres
Tom Harvey	– 4.51 metres
Terry Jackson	– 3.90 metres
Mark Taylor	– 4.19 metres
Luke Webb	– 3.54 metres
Scott Williams	– 3.22 metres

1st = first 2nd = second 3rd = third 4th = fourth
5th = fifth 6th = sixth 7th = seventh 8th = eighth

5 Speaking: Do you like sports?

a) *Act the dialogue with a partner.*

A: What's your favourite sport?
B: It's tennis. I love it.
A: Do you watch it on TV?
B: Yes, I do. I often watch tennis at the weekend.
A: What's your favourite competition?
B: Wimbledon.
A: Who's your favourite star?
B: Venus Williams.

b) *Make new dialogues.*

Say the name of a sport.

Say the name of a competition.

Say the name of a star.

6 School discos

There are lots of discos at Thomas Tallis. *Say why pupils like them.*

1. dance and talk/with friends/pupils
   Pupils dance and talk with friends.
2. always/the DJ/cool music/plays
   Go on, please.
3. karaoke/sing/often/Emma and her friends
4. dance/never/the teachers
5. drinks/sell/pupils from Year 11
6. trouble/at discos/always/there isn't

TIPP

Tipp: Umgang mit neuen Wörtern
Gehe mit deinen neuen Wörtern sorgfältig um. Schreibe ein neues Wort sofort auf, sprich es fünfmal laut und lerne den Beispielsatz. Wiederhole ihn am nächsten Tag. Versuche das mit den Wörtern auf dieser Seite.

7 Word web

Make a word web for 'the school year' in your exercise book.

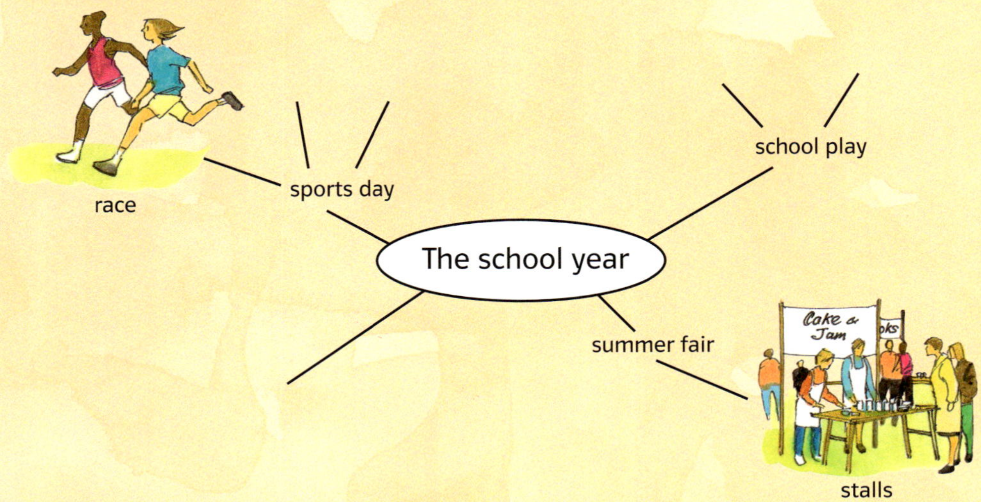

8 Listen and speak

[ɔː]
In the morning
four small boys with a ball
are walking and talking.
That's all.

[ɒ]
The coffee is hot
so give me a lot,
and a box of chocolates, too.
The dog has got my shoe.

9 The months

What are the months?

1. We write four months the same as in German.
2. Four months have the letter 'y'.
3. Three months have the letter 'c'.
4. Only one month has the letter 'h'.

10 What's the date today?

Can you say these dates?

1. "Today is Friday, the twenty-fourth of April."
2. "Today is … ." *Go on, please.*

1. Fri, 24.04.	4. Wed, 7/7
2. Tue, 01.05.	5. Thur, 24/12
3. Sat, 28.02.	6. Mon, 1/1

11 Speaking: Your sports day

a) *Match the words.*

act	the times
take	the sandwiches
do	the discus
run	in a race
throw	in the play
make	the long jump

b) *Talk about what you can do.*

A: What can I do?
B: You can take the times.
C: What can I do?

Go on, please.

12 Picture words

Here are more picture words. Make picture words with the words 'stall', 'spring' and 'lantern'.

13 A song: Hello – Goodbye

You say yes, I say no,
You say stop, and I say go, go, go!
Oh. Oh, no!
You say goodbye, and I say hello.

Hello, hello!
I don't know why you say goodbye,
I say hello!

I say high, you say low,
You say, why? – and I say I don't know!
Oh. Oh, no!
You say goodbye, and I say hello.

Hello, hello!
I don't know why you say goodbye,
I say hello!

Words and music by John Lennon and Paul McCartney

stop – *anhalten*; high – *hoch*; low – *niedrig*

Present progressive *(Verlaufsform in der Gegenwart)*

• present progressive mit *I*

Aussage	**I'm watching** the tennis game. **I'm drinking** tea.	***Ich sehe gerade*** *das Tennisspiel an.* ***Ich trinke gerade*** *Tee.*
Verneinung	**I'm not listening** to music. **I'm not doing** my homework.	***Ich höre gerade nicht*** *Musik.* ***Ich mache gerade nicht*** *meine Hausaufgaben.*
Ja/Nein-Frage	**Are you helping** Mrs Carter? – **Yes, I am.** – **No, I'm not.**	***Hilfst du gerade*** *Mrs Carter?* ***– Ja.*** ***– Nein.***
wh-Frage	What **are you doing?**	*Was* ***machst du gerade?***

• present progressive mit *he/she*

Aussage	**She's taking** the times. **He's helping** her.	***Sie stoppt gerade*** *die Zeit.* ***Er hilft*** *ihr* ***gerade.***
Verneinung	**She isn't listening.** **He isn't watching.**	***Sie hört gerade nicht zu.*** ***Er schaut gerade nicht zu.***
Ja/Nein-Frage	**Is he throwing** the discus? – **Yes, he is.** – **No, he isn't.**	***Ist er gerade*** *beim Diskuswerfen?* ***– Ja.*** ***– Nein.***
wh-Frage	What **is she doing?**	*Was* ***macht sie gerade?***

Cartoon: I'm drinking tea!

Cartoon: She's taking the times.

Checklist

Ich kann	
... fragen, was jemand gerade tut.	What are you doing?
... fragen, was andere gerade tun.	Are they running in a race?
... fragen, was jemand gern tun würde.	What would you like to do?
... fragen, wann etwas stattfindet.	When's the disco?
... sagen, wann etwas stattfindet.	It's on Saturday.
... fragen, wann etwas anfängt.	When does it start?
... sagen, wann etwas anfängt.	It starts at 8 o'clock.
... fragen, wer welche Rolle hat.	Who's the DJ?
... sagen, wer welche Rolle hat.	Peter is the DJ.
... fragen, wer eingeladen ist.	Who can come?
... sagen, wer eingeladen ist.	Everybody can come.
... sagen, welchen Platz jemand belegt.	Tom is first./Simon is second.

Checkout: The two hikers

One day two hikers are in the forest when they see a bear.
The bear starts to chase them.
They run as fast as they can, but the bear is faster.
He gets nearer and nearer.
Suddenly one of the hikers stops and sits down.
He takes off his heavy hiking boots and puts on a pair of trainers.
"Do you really think you can run faster than the bear in those?" asks his friend.
"I don't have to run faster than the bear. I just have to run faster than you!"

Zum Abschluss des Buchs geht es noch einmal zurück zur Natur. Dass Ausflüge dorthin ihre Tücken haben können, siehst du hier. Hier gibt es wieder einige Wörter und Wendungen, die du nicht kennst. Du kannst sie in der alphabetischen Wortliste nachschlagen oder aus dem Zusammenhang erschließen.

TIPP

Tipps: The two hikers

1. faster, nearer: *Beide Wörter sind Steigerungsformen. Die Grundformen heißen* fast *und* near.
2. as fast as: *Adjektive treten oft in Vergleichsformen auf. Dies ist die Vergleichsform von* fast.
3. have to, don't have to: Have to *ist eine andere Ausdrucksmöglichkeit von* must. *Die Verneinung beider Wörter ist gleich.*

A story with photos

1 Terry and the letter

Which picture is it?

1. Mrs Jackson wants to talk to Terry.
   – That's picture 5.
2. The other friends are in the café, too.
   Go on, please.
3. The friends can see Terry with the letter.
4. Sport isn't fun now.
5. Emma is 'worried' about Terry.
6. Terry has got a letter.

2 Happy or angry?

a) *There are two endings[5]. What's different in 7a and 7b?*
b) *Which is your favourite ending, 7a or 7b?*
c) *Write a dialogue and a sentence for your favourite ending.*

On Monday Terry always trains for the basketball team.

Wednesday, in the cafeteria.

Then …

Or …

[1]letter – *Brief*
[2]Pardon? – *Bitte?*
[3]rings – *klingelt*
[4]over there – *dort drüben*
[5]ending – *Ende*

Christmas

All about Christmas[1]

Christmas Eve[2] is 24th December. The children wait for Father Christmas and hang up[3] their stockings[4]. Christmas Day[5] – the big day – is 25th December. In the morning, the children get their presents. There's a big meal on this day: turkey[6] with roast potatoes[7] and vegetables. After that, people eat Christmas pudding[8]. But the best thing about Christmas is the crackers[9]. People pull[10] crackers and find games and funny hats in them. 26th December is Boxing Day[11]. People meet and play or go out together.

[1] Christmas – *Weihnachten;* [2] Christmas Eve – *Heiligabend;* [3] hang up – *aufhängen;* [4] stocking – *Strumpf;* [5] Christmas Day – *erster Weihnachtsfeiertag;* [6] turkey – *Truthahn;* [7] roast potatoes – *Bratkartoffeln;* [8] Christmas pudding – *Plumpudding;* [9] cracker – *Knallbonbon;* [10] pull – *ziehen;* [11] Boxing Day – *zweiter Weihnachtsfeiertag*

A Christmas song: We wish[1] you a merry[2] Christmas

[1] wish – *wünschen;* [2] merry – *fröhlich*

Vocabulary

Auf den „*Vocabulary*"-Seiten findest du alle Wörter und Wendungen in der Reihenfolge, in der sie in *Let's go 1* vorkommen. In der linken Spalte steht das englische Wort, in der Mitte die deutsche Übersetzung und rechts ein Beispielsatz, eine Abbildung oder eine Sammelbox. Fett gedruckte Wörter musst du auf jeden Fall lernen. Schwach gedruckte Wörter benötigst du nur für das Verständnis einzelner Texte in *Let's go 1*. Wenn du wissen willst, wie ein Wort ausgesprochen wird, schaust du in der *Alphabetical word list* ab S. 145 nach. Dort findest du alle Wörter in *Let's go* in alphabetischer Reihenfolge mit der sogenannten Lautschrift. Die Lautschrift zeigt dir, wie Wörter ausgesprochen werden. Hier ist eine Liste der wichtigsten Lautschriftzeichen.

Englische Laute (English sounds)

Selbstlaute (Vowels)

[ɑː]	c**ar**, f**a**ther; ähnlich wie in *Bahn*
[ʌ]	n**u**mber, b**u**s, m**o**ther; ähnlich wie in *Dach*
[e]	y**e**s, p**e**n, fr**ie**nd; ähnlich wie in *nett*
[ə]	**a** book, **a** pen; ähnlich wie der Endlaut in *bitte*
[ɜː]	g**ir**l, h**er**
[æ]	b**a**g, m**a**p, th**a**t
[ɪ]	**i**t, l**i**st, s**i**x; ähnlich wie in *Kind*
[iː]	sh**e**, s**ee**, pl**ea**se; ähnlich wie in *tief*
[ɒ]	**o**n, d**o**g, wh**a**t; ähnlich wie in *Kopf*
[ɔː]	m**or**ning, h**or**se, f**our**; ähnlich wie in *Horn*, aber lang
[ʊ]	p**u**t, l**oo**k, b**oo**k; ähnlich wie in *Schutt*
[uː]	y**ou**, tw**o**, bl**ue**; ähnlich wie in *du*

Doppellaute (Diphtongs)

[ai]	b**i**ro, f**i**ve, m**y**; ähnlich wie in *kein*
[aʊ]	p**ou**nd, n**ow**; ähnlich wie in *Frau*
[eə]	th**ere**, ch**air**, th**eir**
[eɪ]	n**a**me, s**ay**, t**a**ble
[iə]	h**ere**, h**ear**
[ɔɪ]	b**oy**; ähnlich wie in *Heu*
[əʊ]	g**o**, kn**ow**, r**oa**d
[ʊə]	y**our**

Mitlaute (Consonants)

[j]	**y**es, **y**ou; wie das deutsche *j* in ***j**a*
[l]	**l**et's, b**l**ue; schoo**l**, twe**l**ve
[ŋ]	morni**ng**, so**ng**; wie in *si**ng**en*, kein [g] sprechen!
[ŋg]	E**ng**lish, E**ng**land; wie in [ŋ], jedoch mit nachfolgendem [g]
[r]	**r**uler, **r**ed, **r**oad
[s]	**s**ee, **s**i**s**ter; stimmloses, d. h. hartes s wie in *rei**ß**en*
[z]	i**s**, dog**s**, car**s**, stimmhaftes, d. h. weiches s wie in *brau**s**en*
[ʒ]	televi**s**ion; wie in *Jalousie* und *Gelee*
[dʒ]	**G**ermany, **j**eans; wie in ***Dsch**ungel*
[ʃ]	**sh**e, sta**t**ion; wie in *Ti**sch***
[tʃ]	**ch**ild, tea**ch**er; wie in *deu**tsch***
[ð]	**th**e, **th**is, mo**th**er; stimmhafter, d. h. weicher Lispellaut
[θ]	**th**ank you, **Th**ursday; stimmloser, d. h. harter Lispellaut
[v]	**v**olleyball, **v**ideo, o**f**; wie in ***W**asser*
[w]	**o**ne, **wh**at, sand**w**ich
[:]	bedeutet, dass der vorangehende Laut lang ist, z. B. you [juː]
[']	bedeutet, dass die folgende Silbe betont ist, z. B. hello [hə'ləʊ]

Das englische Alphabet (The English alphabet)

a	[eɪ]	**b**	[biː]	**c**	[siː]	**d**	[diː]	**e**	[iː]
f	[ef]	**g**	[dʒiː]	**h**	[eitʃ]	**i**	[aɪ]	**j**	[dʒeɪ]
k	[keɪ]	**l**	[el]	**m**	[em]	**n**	[en]	**o**	[əʊ]
p	[piː]	**q**	[kjuː]	**r**	[ɑː]	**s**	[es]	**t**	[tiː]
u	[juː]	**v**	[viː]	**w**	['dʌbljuː]	**x**	[eks]		
y	[waɪ]	**z**	[zed]						

Let's start

8	let's start	los geht's	
	this is	dies ist, das ist	
	this	dieser, diese, dieses	
	is	ist	
	in	in, im	
	a	ein/eine	
	new	neu	a *new* computer shop
	computer	Computer	
	shop	Laden, Geschäft	
	and	und	Terry *and* Sam
	girl	Mädchen	⚠ Englische Hauptwörter schreibt man klein: *girl*. Nur Namen schreibt man groß: *London*.
	Hello.	Hallo.	*Hello. I'm* Tim. – *Hello. I'm* Kim.
	I'm	Ich bin	
	I	ich	⚠ Das Wort *I* = 'ich' schreibt man immer groß.
	What's your name?	Wie heißt du?	*What's your name?* – I'm Emma.
	what	was	
	name	Name	
	My name is	Ich heiße	*My name is* Emma. = I'm Emma.
	fan	Fan	
9	**eleven**	elf	
	I'm from	Ich komme aus	*I'm from* London.
	from	aus, von	
	mouse	Maus	Tom is a *mouse*.
	one	eins	
	too	auch	
	Say it!	Sag es!	
	How old are you?	Wie alt bist du?	*How old are you?* – I'm eleven.
	Where are you from?	Woher kommst du?	*Where are you from?* – I'm from Stuttgart.
	you	du	I'm Sam. And *you*?
	listening	Hören; *(hier:)* Hörübung	
	the	der, die, das	
	right	richtig	
	order	Reihenfolge	
	go on	mach weiter/macht weiter	
	please	bitte	
	name card	Namensschild	
	let's	lass uns/lasst uns	
	make	machen	
	card	Karte; *(hier:)* Namensschild	
	listen	hör zu/hört zu	
	speak	sprich/sprecht	
	my	mein, meine	Emma: Terry is *my* friend.
	number	Nummer	
	oh	null	
	your	dein/deine	What's *your* name? *My* name is Tim.

Numbers 1

1	one	[wʌn]	**7**	seven	['sevn]
2	two	[tu:]	**8**	eight	[eɪt]
3	three	[θri:]	**9**	nine	[naɪn]
4	four	[fɔ:]	**10**	ten	[ten]
5	five	[faɪv]	**11**	eleven	[ɪ'levn]
6	six	[sɪks]	**12**	twelve	[twelv]

9	**telephone**	Telefon	My *telephone number* is two – seven – *oh* – five.
10	**she**	sie	This is Lisa. *She*'s eleven.
	chatterbox	Plappermaul	
	friend	Freund/Freundin	Lisa is a *friend*. And Terry is a *friend*, too.
	he	er	
	cool	prima, cool	
	music	Musik	
	or	oder	
	boy	Junge	Lisa is a girl. Terry is a *boy*.
	speaking	Sprechen; *(hier:)* Sprechübung	
	introduce	stelle vor/stellt vor	
	Nice to meet you.	Schön dich kennen zu lernen.	
11	**What colour is ...?**	Welche Farbe hat...?	
	what	welcher/welche/welches	
	monster	Monster, Ungeheuer	What colour is the *monster*? – It's blue.
	it	es	
	red	rot	
	yellow	gelb	
	brown	braun	
	pink	pink, rosa	My name card is *pink*.
	blue	blau	
	big	groß	
	green	grün	
	... is after you	... verfolgt dich, ... ist hinter dir her	
	are	bist	
	game	Spiel	

Fragen und Antworten

What's your name?	I'm Emma. / My name is ....
How old are you?	I'm eleven. / ....
Where are you from?	I'm from Frankfurt.
What's your telephone number?	My number is five – oh – three – ....
What colour is the name card / ...?	It's red.

Unit 1: Thomas Tallis School

12	unit	Kapitel	
	intro	Einleitung	
	school	Schule	⚠ Das 'sch' wird 'sk' ausgesprochen, wie bei Skateboard.
	everybody	jeder	Sam, Terry, Lisa, Emma, ... – *everybody*
	Year 7	Klasse sieben	
	the	der, die, das	
	uniform	Uniform	This is my *school uniform*.
	Good morning.	Guten Morgen.	
	here	hier	Where's Terry? – *Here!*

12	**Mrs**	*(Anrede)* Frau	*Mrs* Carter. She's a *teacher*.
	teacher	Lehrer/Lehrerin	
	classroom	Klassenzimmer	
	Mr	*(Anrede)* Herr	*Mr* Newman? He's the *caretaker*.
	caretaker	Hausmeister/ Hausmeisterin	
	that	das; jener, jene, jenes	2 + 2 = 5? *That's wrong*!
	wrong	falsch	⚠ Das 'w' hört man nicht.
13	**are**	sind, seid	
	they	*(pl.)* sie	*They* are new.
	at	in, auf, an, bei	*at* Thomas Tallis School
	you	*(pl.)* ihr	*You* are new. Hello.
	yes	ja	Teacher: Are you Sam? – Sam: *Yes*, I am. 
	we	wir	*We* are new.
	How are you?	Wie geht's?	
	Fine, thanks.	Danke, gut.	
	word	Wort	
	old	alt	

Language

14	language	Sprache	
	pupil	Schüler/Schülerin	Sam is *a pupil*.
	tutor group	Klasse *(in einer englischen Schule)*	
	group	Gruppe	
	where	wo	*Where's* Lisa? – She's here. ⚠ where's = where is
	no	Nein	Are you Lisa? – *No*, I'm *not*. I'm Emma.
	not	nicht	
	Oh.	Oh.	
	chair	Stuhl	
	What's wrong?	Was ist los?	*What's wrong*? 
	OK	OK; in Ordnung	
	thank you	danke (schön)	Here's a computer game. – *Thank you*.
	but	aber	This chair is new, *but* this chair is old.  
	What's missing?	Was fehlt?	
	make	mache/macht	
	dialogue	Dialog, Gespräch	
	with	mit	
	partner	Partner/Partnerin	
15	**I've got**	ich habe, ich besitze	*I've got* a blue bag. = This is my bag.
	have got	haben, besitzen	
	pencil	Bleistift	
	pencil case	Federmäppchen	
	exercise book	Übungsheft	
	bag	Tasche	
	book	Buch, Heft	
	ruler	Lineal	
	rubber	Radiergummi	
	pen	Füller	
	felt-tip	Filzstift	

In the pencil case
felt-tip, ruler, rubber, pencil, pen

In the bag
pencil case, exercise book, books

15	**picture**	Bild	
	broken	kaputt	The chair is *broken*.
	let's	lass/lasst uns	
	find	finden	*Let's find* Terry!
	who	wer	*Who's* Mrs Carter? – She's a teacher. ⚠ who's = who is
	Germany	Deutschland	
16	**there**	da, dort	Sam isn't *there*. He's here.
	board	Tafel, Anschlagtafel	**In the classroom** window, board, table,
	window	Fenster	
	table	Tisch	
	spell	buchstabiere/ buchstabiert	
	star	Star, Stern	
17	**modern**	modern	a new school = a *modern* school
	library	Bücherei, Bibliothek	Books are in the *library*. ⚠ Der Teil 'li' reimt sich mit dem Wort 'my'.
	sports hall	Turnhalle	
	cafeteria	Cafeteria	
	room	Zimmer, Raum	A *room* is in a house.
	an	ein/eine	a picture, *an* e-mail
	e-mail	E-Mail	
	to	an, nach, zu	an *e-mail to* Emma from Lisa
	we've got	wir haben, wir besitzen	Emma and Lisa: *We've got* a computer.
	text	Text	

At Thomas Tallis School

classrooms	library
computer room	cafeteria
sports hall	shop

Text: Friends

18	**lunch break**	Mittagspause	
	lunch	Mittagessen	
	with	mit, mit ... zusammen, bei	Terry is *with* Sam and Lisa.
	listen	zuhören, anhören	
	joke	Witz	Ha, ha, ha! *a joke*
	word	Wort	
	twenty-six	sechsundzwanzig	A = 1; B = 2; ... .. Z = *twenty-six*
	letter	Buchstabe	The *word* 'joke' has got 4 *letters*.
	easy	einfach	1 + 1 = ? – That's *easy*: 2!
	alphabet	Alphabet	A, B, C, D, ... That's the *alphabet*.
	right	richtig	2 + 2 = 4. – *Right!*
	boring	langweilig	Good book? – No, it's *boring*.
	all	alle, alles	
	Goodbye.	Auf Wiedersehen.	
	outside	außen, draußen, außerhalb	in the classroom – *outside*
	now	jetzt, nun	⚠ *Now* reimt sich mit dem Wort 'how'.
	ball	Ball	
	good	gut	
	good at	gut in	
	sports	Sport	I'm *good at sports*.
	problem	Problem	
19	**I'm sorry.**	Tut mir Leid.	*I'm sorry.*

19	**please**	bitte	My ball, *please*. – Thank you.
	Here you are.	Hier bitte.	Where's my pen? – *Here you are.*
	play	spielen	I've got a ball. Let's *play*.

Practice

20	practice	Übung	
	match to	ordne zu/ordnet zu	
21	project	Projekt	
	poster	Poster	

Words

22	list	Liste	
	for	für	A book *for* you. – Thank you.
	word web	Wortnetz	

Grammar

24	grammar	Grammatik	

Let's check

25	check	prüfen, kontrollieren	
	checklist	Checkliste, Kontrollliste	
	checkout	Abschlusskontrolle, Auschecken	

Lerncheck Unit 1

1. Kannst du diese Wörter richtig aussprechen?

school	uniform
board	modern
right	now
wrong	library

2. Welche Wörter fehlen?

from in at

1. Lisa and Emma are ... Greenwich.
2. They're ... Thomas Tallis School.
3. The school is ... Greenwich.
4. The girls are ... Year 7.
5. Lisa is good ... sports.

Bridge 1: A house for a mouse

26	**bridge**	Brücke	
	house	Haus	
	bathroom	Badezimmer	
	bedroom	Schlafzimmer	
	kitchen	Küche	Here's Tom. He is in the *kitchen*.
	dining room	Esszimmer	
	living room	Wohnzimmer	
	TV	Fernseher	
	bed	Bett	The *bed* is in the bedroom.
	sofa	Sofa	
	cupboard	Küchenschrank, Schrank	⚠ Das 'p' wird nicht ausgesprochen.

In a room
TV, bed, sofa, cupboard

26	**cheese**	Käse	
	game	Spiel	
	cat	Katze	
	rucksack	Rucksack	⚠ Achte auf die Aussprache! – das 'u' und das 'a' spricht man anders aus als im Deutschen.
	his	sein/seine	
27	**van**	Lieferwagen, Kleintransporter	
	rap	Rap	

Unit 2: At home

28	**at home**	zu Hause, daheim	Tom is in his house. = Tom is *at home*. 
	garden	Garten	
	tree	Baum	two *trees*
	shed	Schuppen	A *shed* is in the *garden*.
	meeting place	Treffpunkt	
	for	für	
	family	Familie	This is my *family*.
	mother	Mutter	
	father	Vater	
	sister	Schwester	my *father*, my *mother*, my *sister*
	or	oder	
	flat	Wohnung	
	over	über	The *flat* is *over* the shop.
29	**brother**	Bruder	Ben is Lisa's *brother*.
	dog	Hund	
	grandma	Oma	
	car	Auto	

Language

30	**Friday**	Freitag	
	after	nach	
	act	spiele/spielt	
	ask	frage/fragt	
	class	Schulklasse, Klasse	
31	**small**	klein	a *small* dog, a big dog  
	she has got	sie hat, sie besitzt	
	her	ihr/ihre	Lisa has got *her own* room.
	own	eigener/eigene/eigenes	
	tidy	sauber, ordentlich	
	comic	Comicheft	
	radio	Radio	Nasreen is a music fan. She's got a *radio*.
	say	sage/sagt	
	nice	nett, schön	
	great	großartig	Is Terry's shed good? – Yes, it's *great*!
	crazy	verrückt	
	thing	Ding, Sache	
32	**India**	Indien	
	nurse	Krankenpfleger/Krankenschwester	two *nurses* 

32	**English**	Engländer/Engländerin	Sam is from London. He's *English*.
	talk about	sprich über/ sprecht über	
	is/are fun	macht/machen Spaß	*It's fun* with friends. Computers *are fun*, too.
	can	können	I *can read* books. 
	read	lesen	
	watch	anschauen, zusehen	They can *watch* TV. 
	cartoon	Cartoon, Zeichentrickfilm	
	listen to	hören, anhören	*Listen* to this! 
	drums	Schlagzeug	
	party	Party	
	have a party	eine Party feiern	
	do	tun, machen	What can you *do* at home? – I can read comics, I can watch TV ....
	CD	CD	
33	**on Sunday**	am Sonntag; sonntags	
	on	am, auf	
	Sunday	Sonntag	
	can't	nicht können	
	breakfast	Frühstück	
	tea	Tee	
	give	geben, schenken	Can you *give me the tea*, please? – Here you are. – Thank you.
	me	mir; mich	**Things for breakfast** tea, butter, coffee, cornflakes, toast, egg, milk
	butter	Butter	
	coffee	Kaffee	
	cornflakes	Cornflakes	
	toast	Toast(brot)	
	egg	Ei	
	milk	Milch	
	awful	furchtbar, scheußlich	He's great. – No, he isn't. He's *awful*!

Text: The room

34	**Saturday**	Samstag	
	homework	Hausaufgaben	
	angry	zornig, wütend	 
	That's that!	Damit basta!	
	happy	glücklich, froh	She's *angry*, but he's *happy*.
	talk about	sprechen über, reden über	
	maybe	vielleicht	Is Sam eleven? – *Maybe*. *Maybe* he's twelve.
	help	helfen	I can do my *homework* with my friend. He can *help* me. 
	again	wieder	
	be **lucky**	Glück haben	*I'm lucky*. I've got two great brothers.
35	be **worried**	beunruhigt sein, besorgt sein	Are you happy? No, *I'm worried*.
	go on	weitermachen, weitergehen	
	idea	Idee	I've got an *idea*! 

35	**rule**	Regel	
	make	machen, tun	I haven't got a nice poster for my room. – We can *make* a poster.
	Be quiet.	Sei leise./Seid leise.	*Be quiet!*
	be	sein	
	quiet	leise	
	people	Leute, Menschen	

Practice

36	**skateboard**	Skateboard	
37	look at	sieh an/seht an, schau an/schaut an	
	write	schreibe/schreibt	
	question	Frage	
	draw	zeichnen	*Draw* a picture with a pencil.
	football	Fußball	I've got a ball. We can play *football*.

Words

38	answer	beantworte/beantwortet	
	in English	auf Englisch	
	poster	Poster	
39	how many	wie viele	
	apple	Apfel	a tree, an *apple*

Lerncheck Unit 2

Welche Wörter fehlen? do have listen to read watch make

1. I can … a book.
2. I can … music.
3. I can … my homework.
4. I can … TV.
5. I can … a party.
6. I can … breakfast.

Bridge 2: Hobbies

42	hobby	Hobby	
	basketball	Basketball	
	guitar	Gitarre	I can play the *guitar* and I can play *tennis*, too!
	tennis	Tennis	
	rabbit	Kaninchen	
	frog	Frosch	
	fish	Fisch	
	guinea pig	Meerschweinchen	
	bird	Vogel	
	favourite	Lieblings-	I like basketball, and I like tennis, too. But my *favourite* sport is football.
	animal	Tier	
43	**pet**	Haustier	
	say	sagen	

Animals
rabbit, frog, fish, guinea pig, bird, cat, dog, mouse

Unit 3: Fun with the friends

44	**school team**	Schulmannschaft	
	train	trainieren	I'm in the *school team*. We *train* in the sports hall.
	Monday	Montag	It's *Monday*. We watch basketball *on Monday*.
	Thursday	Donnerstag	
	go jogging	joggen gehen	
	Wednesday	Mittwoch	⚠ Der Teil 'Wednes' reimt sich mit dem Wort 'pens'.
	go swimming	schwimmen gehen	
	Tuesday	Dienstag	*Tuesday* – Thursday ⚠ Achte auf den Unterschied!
	part	Teil	
	sentence	Satz	
45	**sing**	singen	
	karaoke	Karaoke	
	dance	tanzen	I *sing karaoke*. – And I *dance*. 
	boy band	Boy Group	
	like	mögen, gern haben	I *like* basketball. – And I *like* Robbie Williams.
	Formula One	Formel Eins	*Formula One* is great! 
	card trick	Kartentrick	
	practise	üben	I play football. I train on Tuesday. – I play the drums. I *practise* on Monday, Tuesday, Wednesday .... 
	weekend	Wochenende	
	at the weekend	am Wochenende	on Saturday, on Sunday = *at the weekend*

Language

46	**cousin**	Cousin/Cousine, Vetter	
	work	arbeiten	
	galaxy	Galaxie, Milchstraße	
	young	jung	Is the nurse *young*? – No, she's old.
	people	Leute, Menschen	There's not one man or woman, there are ten *people*.
	always	immer	
	programme	Sendung	How's the *programme*? – It's boring.
	from ... to	von ... bis	
	never	nie, niemals	
	sometimes	manchmal	
	talk to	sprechen mit, reden mit	
	pop star	Popstar	
	send	schicken, senden	
	every	jeder/jede/jedes	I have breakfast *every* day.
	day	Tag	
	often	oft	
	phone	anrufen	
	on the programme	in der Sendung	
	quiz	Quiz	
47	**go**	gehen, fahren	
	him	ihm; ihn	
	today	heute	
	survey	Umfrage	
	about	über	

Go or play?

go ...	play ...
jogging	games
swimming	basketball
to the park	in a team
home	the drums
to bed	in a band

47	**buy**	kaufen	You can *buy* CDs in a shop.
	then	dann	
48	**Hi.**	Hallo.	Hello, Sam! – *Hi*, Terry!
	your	euer/eure, Ihr/Ihre	
	DJ	Diskjockey	
	our	unser/unsere	This is *our* computer. – I like *your* computer.
	caller	Anrufer/Anruferin	
	very	sehr	
	you	dir; dich	
	song	Lied	Let's sing a *song*.
	their	ihr; ihre	*Their* computer is cool!
	start	anfangen	
	ask	fragen	
49	**park**	Park	
	there is	da ist, es gibt, es ist	*There is* a big tree in the park.
	man *pl.* **men**	Mann	a *man* and two girls
	balloon	Luftballon	
	there are	da sind	*There are* four boys, too.
	bingo	Bingospiel	

Numbers 2

13	thirteen	[θɜːˈtiːn]	**21**	twenty-one	[twentiˈwʌn]	**30**	thirty	[ˈθɜːti]
14	fourteen	[fɔːˈtiːn]	**22**	twenty-two	[twentiˈtuː]	**40**	forty	[ˈfɔːti]
15	fifteen	[fɪfˈtiːn]	**23**	…		**50**	fifty	[ˈfɪfti]
16	sixteen	[sɪksˈtiːn]	…			**60**	sixty	[ˈsɪksti]
17	seventeen	[sevnˈtiːn]				**70**	seventy	[ˈsevnti]
18	eighteen	[eɪˈtiːn]				**80**	eighty	[ˈeɪti]
19	nineteen	[nainˈtiːn]				**90**	ninety	[ˈnainti]
20	twenty	[ˈtwenti]				**100**	one hundred	[wʌnˈhʌndrəd]

Text: Barker's story

50	story	Geschichte	
	children *(pl.)*	Kinder	two girls and three boys = five *children*
	job	Arbeit, Beruf	Man: What's your *job*? – Teacher: I'm a teacher.
	morning	Morgen, Vormittag	
	in the morning	am Morgen; morgens	
	get up	aufstehen	Terry! *Get up*, please!
	wash	waschen	
	face	Gesicht	a happy *face*, an angry *face*, a crazy *face*
	then	dann	
	have breakfast	frühstücken	I get up, *then* I *have breakfast*.
	take	nehmen, mitnehmen	Oh no! My pen is broken! – Here, *take* my felt-tip.
	get lost	sich verlaufen	
	call	rufen, anrufen	
	home	nach Hause	
	evening	Abend	
51	**in the evening**	am Abend; abends	Tom in the morning, Tom *in the evening*.
	sit	sitzen	
	in front of	vor	Tom is *in front of* a house.
	throw	werfen	

51	**shoe**	Schuh	
	go out	ausgehen, ausfahren	
	road	Straße	The cars are on the *road*. 
	bark	bellen	
	long	lang	
	tired	müde	
	go to bed	schlafen gehen, ins Bett gehen	
	sleep	schlafen	Lisa and Barker are very *tired*. = They are *dog-tired*. They can *sleep*. 
	dog-tired	hundemüde	
	when	wann	

Practice

52	put together	lege zusammen/ legt zusammen	
	think	finden, meinen, denken	
53	**player**	Spieler/Spielerin	
	hockey	Hockey	
	team	Mannschaft, Team	Are you in the school *team*? – No, I'm in the Year 7 *team*.
	See you there.	Wir sehen uns dort.	We train at the sports hall. – OK. *See you there*. Bye!
	see	sehen	

Words

54	**hobby**	Hobby	
	pair	Paar	
55	write down	schreibe auf/schreibt auf	
	last	letzter/letzte/letztes	

Lerncheck Unit 3

1. Welche Tage fehlen?

a) Monday … Wednesday
b) Sunday … Tuesday
c) Tuesday … Thursday
d) Thursday … Saturday

2. Welche Buchstaben fehlen?

You can **go** j…ing
sw…ing
to the p…k
ho…
to b…

Bridge 3: In town

In town
post office, café, market, sports hall, school, poster shop, sports shop, music shop, bookshop, computer shop

58	**in town**	in der Stadt	
	town	Stadt	
	post office	Postamt	
	car park	Parkplatz	There's a big *car park* for 100 cars in town.
	café	Café	
	market	Markt	
	next to	neben	Tom is *next to* Susie. 
	opposite	gegenüber (von)	Now Tom is *opposite* Susie. 

58	**clock**	Uhr	
	What time is it?	Wie viel Uhr ist es?	What *time* is it? – Look at the *clock*!
	time	Zeit	
	... o'clock	... Uhr	It's three *o'clock*.
	past	nach	It's ten *past* four.
	quarter past	viertel nach	⚠ Der Teil 'quar' reimt sich mit dem Wort 'four'.
	half past	halb	*half past* four = four thirty
	to	*(hier:)* vor	
59	**meet**	treffen, sich treffen, kennen lernen	Let's *meet* at twenty *to* five.

Unit 4: In Greenwich

60	**interesting**	interessant	This book isn't boring. It's very *interesting*.
	part	Teil	
	of	von	
	bus	Bus	
	by (bus)	mit (dem Bus)	
	train	Zug	
	Underground	U-Bahn	
	look	sehen, schauen	*Look left! Look right!*
	left	links	
	west	Westen	
	right	rechts	
	east	Osten	
	north	Norden	
	south	Süden	
	Royal Observatory	*Observatorium in Greenwich*	
	home	Heim, Zuhause	
	Meridian Line	*Längengrad Null*	
	boat	Boot, Schiff	
	tunnel	Tunnel, Unterführung	
	tourist	Tourist/Touristin	
	walk	gehen, laufen	Sometimes I *walk* to school, sometimes I take the bus.
	under	unter	
	River Thames	Themse *(Fluss in London)*	
	river	Fluss	In London you can see the *river* Thames.
61	**famous**	berühmt	Mickey is a *famous* mouse.
	lots of	viele	I've got *lots of* CDs.

You can go ...
by bus.
by train.
by Underground.
by bike.
by car.
by boat. Or you can walk.

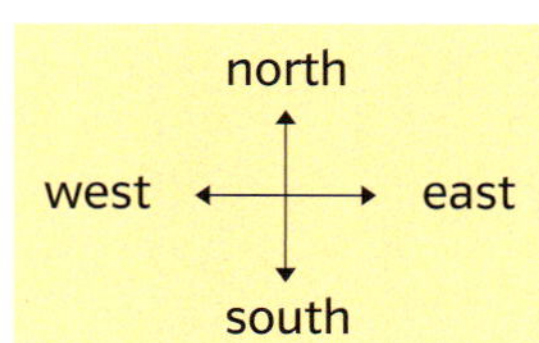

Language

62	**map**	Stadtplan, Landkarte	
	along	entlang	
	turn	abbiegen	
	into	in, hinein	
	straight on	geradeaus	
	on the left	links	

Richtungsangaben
Go along the road.
Go straight on.
Turn left/right into Park Road.
on the left
on the right

62	**Information Centre**	Informationszentrum	
	street	Straße	*street* = road
	Excuse me.	Entschuldigung.	*Excuse me*, please. – Yes, how can I help you?
	on the right	rechts	
63	**take**	nehmen, mit … fahren	Sometimes I *walk* to school, sometimes I *take* the bus.
	week	Woche	A *week* has got seven days.
	look at	anschauen, ansehen	Where's Greenwich? – *Look at* the map.
64	**project day**	Projekttag	
	year	Jahr	Terry is twelve. = He's twelve *years* old. Andreas is in class 5B. = He's in *Year* 5. 
	write	schreiben	I can *write* my name. ⚠ Das *'w'* wird nicht ausgesprochen.
	project	Projekt	
	know	kennen, wissen	I *know* your name. You're Tom. 
	question	Frage	– Right! Now I've got a *question*. What's your name?
	worksheet	Arbeitsblatt	
	why	warum	*Why* is Tom angry? – His skateboard is broken.
	come	kommen	
	how	wie	*How* old is Terry? – He's twelve.
	speak	sprechen	
	German	Deutsch	I can *speak German*. I can say: "Guten Tag!"
	hear	hören	
	the same	derselbe/dieselbe/dasselbe	We've got *the same* name! 
65	**GMT**	*Abkürzung von Greenwich Mean Time*	
	mean	bedeuten, heißen	'Bike' *means* 'Fahrrad' in German.
	meal	Mahlzeit, Essen	Breakfast and lunch are *meals*.
	sure	sicher	Is Dan a famous DJ? – Maybe. I'm not *sure*.
	Greenwich Mean Time	Greenwicher Zeit *(erste Zeitzone)*	
	World Time	Weltzeit	
	work	funktionieren	Does your radio *work*? – No, it's broken.
	answer	Antwort	Father, can we buy a new car? – The *answer* is 'No!'

Text: A cool idea?

66	**at**	*(hier:)* um	
	answer	beantworten, antworten	Can you *answer* the questions? – Yes, I can.
	when	wann	*When* does the computer shop *open*? – At ten o'clock, and it *closes* at seven o'clock. 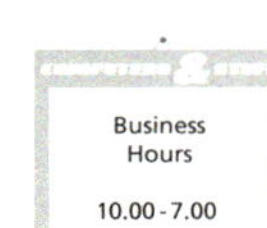
	restaurant	Restaurant, Gaststätte	
	open	öffnen	
	close	schließen	
	information	Information	
	live	wohnen, leben	Our house is in Greenwich. = We *live* in Greenwich.
	so	so	
	make up	erfinden, sich ausdenken	Emma can sing, and she can *make up* new songs, too.

66	**find out**	herausfinden	Sorry, I haven't got the information, but I can *find out* for you.
	lazy	faul	Homework? No, thank you! I'm *lazy*!
	clever	klug	
67	**hard**	schwierig, hart	Our project isn't easy. – It's *hard*.
	ready	fertig	Ben! Jade! Breakfast is *ready*!
	plan	Plan	
	trick	Trick	

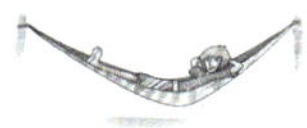

Practice

68	**parents**	Eltern	Your mother and father are your *parents*.
	church	Kirche	We go to *church* on Sunday.
	swimming pool	Schwimmbad	I can go swimming in the *swimming pool*.
69	**bike**	Fahrrad	
	have lunch	zu Mittag essen	

Words

70	sign	Schild, Zeichen	
71	**mobile phone**	Handy, Mobiltelefon	⚠ Vorsicht! Im Englischen sagt man für ein Mobiltelefon nie 'Handy'.
	sweatshirt	Sweatshirt	

Lerncheck Unit 4

Wo gehören die Fragewörter hin? What When Where Who Why

1. … do tourists like Greenwich? – It's interesting.
2. … is the tunnel? – Under the Thames.
3. … does 'berühmt' mean in English? – Famous.
4. … does Emma go to Greenwich? – Every Saturday.
5. … knows all the tricks? – Mr Rose, the teacher.

Bridge 4: Party time!

74	**robot**	Roboter	*Robots* can make cars.
	clown	Clown	
	food	Nahrung, Essen	
	sandwich	Sandwich, belegtes Brot	
	T-shirt	T-Shirt	
	trousers	Hose	⚠ Das Wort *trousers* ist immer Plural. 'Du hast eine neue Hose' heißt auf Englisch: 'You've got new *trousers*'.
	skirt	Rock	She's got a nice *skirt*.
	hat	Hut	
	clothes	Kleider, Kleidung	T-shirts, trousers, skirts, … = *clothes* ⚠ Das Wort *clothes* ist auch immer Plural. Achte auf die Aussprache – nur eine Silbe!

Unit 5: Happy birthday!

76	**Happy birthday!**	Herzlichen Glückwunsch zum Geburtstag!	*Happy birthday!*

Numbers 3

first	[fɜːst]	erste(-r/-s)	**eleventh**	[ɪˈlevnθ]	elfte(-r/-s)
second	[ˈseknd]	zweite(-r/-s)	**twelfth**	[twelfθ]	zwölfte(-r/-s)
third	[θɜːd]	dritte(-r/-s)	**thirteenth**	[θɜːˈtiːnθ]	dreizehnte(-r/-s)
fourth	[fɔːθ]	vierte(-r/-s)	**fourteenth**	[fɔːˈtiːnθ]	vierzehnte(-r/-s)
fifth	[fɪfθ]	fünfte(-r/-s)	**fifteenth**	[fɪfˈtiːnθ]	fünfzehnte(-r/-s)
sixth	[sɪksθ]	sechste(-r/-s)	**sixteenth**	[sɪksˈtiːnθ]	sechzehnte(-r/-s)
seventh	[ˈsevnθ]	siebte(-r/-s)	**seventeenth**	[sevnˈtiːnθ]	siebzehnte(-r/-s)
eighth	[eɪtθ]	achte(-r/-s)	**eighteenth**	[eɪˈtiːnθ]	achzehnte(-r/-s)
ninth	[naɪnθ]	neunte(-r/-s)	**nineteenth**	[naɪnˈtiːnθ]	neunzehnte(-r/-s)
tenth	[tenθ]	zehnte(-r/-s)	**twentieth**	[twentiɪθ]	zwanzigste(-r/-s)

Months

January	[ˈdʒænjʊri]	Januar	**July**	[dʒʊˈlaɪ]	Juli
February	[ˈfebrʊri]	Februar	**August**	[ˈɔːgəst]	August
March	[mɑːtʃ]	März	**September**	[sepˈtembə]	September
April	[ˈeɪprl]	April	**October**	[ɒkˈtəʊbə]	Oktober
May	[meɪ]	Mai	**November**	[nəʊˈvembə]	November
June	[dʒuːn]	Juni	**December**	[dɪˈsembə]	Dezember

	birthday	Geburtstag	
	date	Datum	What's the *date*? – It's 10th September.
	mum	Mama	
	dad	Papa	
	invitation	Einladung	
	Dear	Lieber/Liebe/Liebes *(in Briefanrede)*	⚠ So fängst du einen Brief an: *Dear* Sam, *Dear* Mrs Brook,
77	**get**	bekommen, kriegen	
	card	Karte	
	present	Geschenk	
	I'd like to ….	Ich würde gerne …. / Ich möchte ….	
	cake	Kuchen	a birthday *present*, a birthday *cake*, a birthday *card*
	ice cream	Eis, Eiscreme	

Language

78	**soon**	bald	
	busy	beschäftigt	I must do many things now. I'm *busy*.
	too	zu	
	much	viel	
	stress	Stress, Belastung	Let's have a party with 100 people! – Oh no! That's *too much stress*.

78	**Anything else?**	Sonst noch etwas?	20 exercise books and 10 pencils, please. *Anything else?* – No, thanks, that's all.
	by	von	
	in-line skates	Inline-Skates, Inliner	
	stressed	gestresst, belastet	Dad is worried and tired. = He's *stressed.* I've got too much stress. = I'm *stressed.*
	Would you like ...?	Möchtest du ...?/ Möchten Sie ...?	*Would you like* a sandwich? – Yes, please. *I'd like* an egg sandwich.
	drink	Getränk	milk, tea, coffee = *drinks*
	orange juice	Orangensaft	
	glass	Glas	
79	**these**	diese	Look at *these* in-line skates!
	How much are they?	Wieviel kosten sie?	
	They're	*(hier:)* Sie kosten	*How much are they?* – They're twenty *pounds.* £10 = ten *pounds*
	pound	Pfund *(britische Währungseinheit)*	⚠ Das *pound*-Zeichen steht vor der Zahl.
	expensive	teuer	
80	**really**	wirklich	
	her	ihr; sie	
	tomorrow	morgen	It's Friday. *Tomorrow* is Saturday.
	love	lieben, gern mögen	
	fetch	holen, abholen	I always *fetch* my children from school. 
	us	uns; wir	We can't play this game. Please help *us.*
	also	auch	
	them	sie; ihnen	Lisa and Emma are here. Ask *them.*
	taxi	Taxi	a *taxi*, the *driver* 
81	**driver**	Fahrer/Fahrerin	
	journalist	Journalist/Journalistin	⚠ Der Teil 'jour' wird gesprochen wie 'Ger' in 'German'.
	work	Arbeit	
	finish	beenden	My shop closes at 7 o'clock. And I *finish work* then. 
	have dinner	zu Abend essen	
	dinner	Abendessen	
	How much is it?	Wie viel kostet es?	That's a great bag. *How much is it?*
	It's	*(hier:)* Es kostet	– *It's* five pounds.
	fine	in Ordnung	
	go shopping	einkaufen gehen	I always *go shopping* at the weekend. 

Text: A special present

82	**special**	besonderer, besondere, besonderes	Your birthday is a *special* day. ⚠ Das 'c' wird 'sh' ausgesprochen, wie in dem Wort 'fish'.
	still	noch	Is Lisa twelve? – No, she's *still* eleven.
	because	weil	Why are you so happy, Tom? – *Because* it's my birthday tomorrow.
	sad	traurig, schmerzlich	Emma isn't happy. She's *sad.*
	Come on!	Komm!/Kommt!	
	DVD	DVD	
	back	zurück	
	look for	suchen	Where's my bag? – I don't know. Let's *look for* it.

82	**hot**	heiß	It's *hot*.
	cold	kalt	It's *cold*.

83	**which**	welcher/welche/wel-ches	
	door	Tür	
	attic	Dachboden, Speicher	
	spider	Spinne	
	in there	da drin, dort drin	
	hate	hassen, nicht mögen	Do you like *spiders?* – No, I *hate* them. They're awful!
	this is why	deshalb	Sam has got a present for Emma. *This is why* he's here.
	those	jene	
	design	Muster, Entwurf	Cool T-shirt, Tom. – Yes, it's my own *design*.
	fantastic	fantastisch, toll	
	You're welcome.	Bitte. / Gern geschehen.	

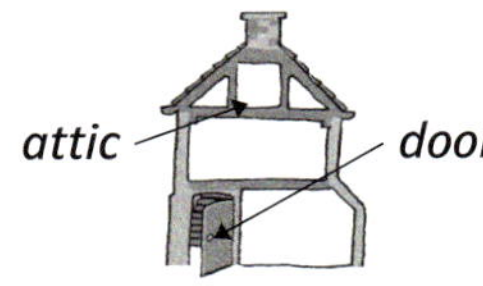

Practice

84	**snack**	Imbiss, Snack	
	funny	komisch, lustig	Do you like my joke? – Ha, ha! Yes, it's very *funny!*
	have a coffee	Kaffee trinken	Mrs Brook *has a coffee* every morning.
85	**photo**	Foto, Fotografie	
	glasses	Brille	⚠ In der Bedeutung 'Brille' wird das Wort *glasses* immer im Plural benutzt.
	cinema	Kino	You can see good *films* at the *cinema* in town.
	film	Film	

Words

86	**thirsty**	durstig	I'd like a big drink. I'm so *thirsty*!

Lerncheck Unit 5

Welche Wörter fehlen?

1. It's my … on Saturday. Can we have a party?
2. Anything …? – Yes, four apples, please.
3. … you like a drink? – Oh, yes, please.
4. How … are the bags? – They're £10.
5. Why are you sad? – … my friends aren't here.

Bridge 5: On the farm

90	**farm**	Bauernhof	
	tractor	Traktor	The *tractor* is in the *field*.
	pond	Teich	Frogs live in *ponds*.
	field	Feld, Acker	
	duck	Ente	
	pony	Pony	⚠ Der Teil 'po' reimt sich mit dem Wort 'no'. Die englische Pluralform heißt *ponies*.
	hen	Henne, Huhn	
	sheep *pl.* **sheep**	Schaf	
	cow	Kuh	
	weather	Wetter	What's the *weather* like? – Awful!

Animals on a farm
pony, hen, duck, cow, sheep

90	**rainy**	regnerisch, verregnet	It's *rainy*. 
	cloudy	bewölkt, wolkig	It's *cloudy*. 
	sunny	sonnig, heiter	It's *sunny*. 

Unit 6: A holiday in Devon

92	**visit**	besuchen	Come and see me here! = Come and *visit* me!
	southwest	südwestlich, Südwest-	
	holiday	Ferien, Urlaub	We always have a *holiday* in July. 
	want to	wollen, mögen	I *want to* eat an ice cream!
	stay	wohnen, übernachten	Come and have a *holiday* in England. You can *stay* in my house!
	activity centre	Freizeitzentrum	
	beach	Strand	
	wild	wild	These ponies don't live on a farm. They're *wild*.
	alone	alleine	This boy isn't with his friends. He's *alone*.
93	**where**	wohin	*Where* can we go? – To the cinema or to the swimming pool.
	hotel	Hotel	

Language

94	**must**	müssen	TV? No, you *must* finish your dinner! 
	careful	vorsichtig	Be *careful*, Terry!
	tell	sagen, erzählen	I know a very funny joke. – Oh, please *tell* me!
	feed	füttern	Barker wants his food. Lisa *feeds* him.
	dangerous	gefährlich	
	leave	verlassen	After the film you *leave* the cinema and go home.
95	**noise**	Geräusch, Lärm	
	woman *pl.* **women**	Frau	
	eat	essen, fressen	I sometimes *eat* apples, and I often *eat* hamburgers.
	men	Männer	one man – two *men*
	repair	reparieren	
	farm machine	landwirtschaftliche Maschine	A tractor is a *farm machine*.
	run	laufen, rennen	Wait! Don't *run*!
	bull	Stier, Bulle	
	behind	hinter	Tom is *behind* the tent.
96	**hope**	hoffen	Hi, Tina. I *hope* you're having a great holiday. 
	so	also, folglich	It's rainy, *so* the children aren't on the beach.
	television	Fernseher	*television* = TV
	vegetable	Gemüse	*vegetables* ⚠ Der Teil 'tables' wird nicht wie das Wort 'tables' = Tische ausgesprochen. 
	hamburger	Hamburger	
97	**tent**	Zelt	
	sleeping bag	Schlafsack	You can sleep in a *sleeping bag*. 
	torch	Taschenlampe	I always sleep with my *torch*.
	some	einige, etwas	I've got six sandwiches, four apples and *some* orange juice.
	water	Wasser	
	knife *pl.* **knives**	Messer	⚠ Das 'k' wird nicht ausgesprochen.

Text: An adventure on the farm

98	adventure	Abenteuer	
	path	Pfad, Weg	
	carry	tragen	Barker can *carry* Lisa's bag!
	large	groß, riesig	*large* = big
	box	Kiste	a *box*, a lot of *boxes* 
	put	setzen, stellen, legen	*Put* the box on the table.
	bush	Busch, Gebüsch	
	drive	fahren	People *drive* a car or a bus – but not a bike.
	away	weg	Don't go *away*! Come back here!
	DVD player	DVD-Spieler	
	video camera	Videokamera, Camcorder	
	criminal	Verbrecher/ Verbrecherin	That boy has got my bike and my mobile phone! He's a *criminal*! 
	follow	folgen	*Follow me*, please!
99	**police**	Polizei	
	police officer	Polizist/Polizistin	
	break-in	Einbruch	It's a *break-in*!
	near	nahe, in der Nähe von	Terry's and Sam's tent is *near* the car park.
	show	zeigen	
	watch	beobachten	

Ähnliche Verben

You **stand** …	in a shop, near the door, behind a tree,	and you **stay** …	in a hotel. at a friend's house. on a farm.
You **listen to** …	CDs, the radio,	and you **hear** …	cars in the road. a cat in the garden.
Your parents **drive** their car,		and you **go** by car.	

Practice

100	**pig**	Schwein	
	wear	anhaben, tragen *(Kleidung)*	You *wear* clothes, but you *carry* bags, books, … .
101	**matchstick people**	*(pl.)* Strichmännchen	
	matchstick man	Strichmännchen	

Lerncheck Unit 6

Welche Wörter fehlen? eat feed put show tell think

1. Cows don't … eggs.
2. I can … you a funny joke.
3. A farmer must … his animals.
4. Please … me your new mobile phone.
5. Many girls … football is boring.
6. … the apples in the box, please.

Unit 7: The school year

106	**autumn**	Herbst	⚠ Vergiss nicht das 'n' am Ende!
	term	Trimester, Semester	
	different	verschieden, anders	D is *different*. 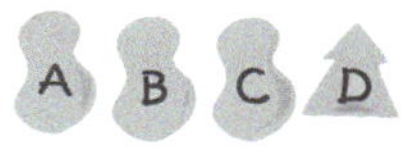
	event	Ereignis, Veranstaltung	
	disco	Disko	You can dance at a *disco*.
	festival	Fest	
	lantern	Laterne	⚠ Vorsicht! Das englische Wort ist ein bisschen anders.
	procession	Umzug, Festzug	
	spring	Frühling	
	play	Spiel, Theaterstück	
	act	spielen *(eine Rolle)*	It's me, Tom. I'm *acting* a cat in a *play*. 
	exchange	Austausch	
	visit	Besuch	We want to visit London; we've got plans for our *visit*.
	take part in	teilnehmen an	Let's *take part in* the class project. – OK, I can make a poster.
	art	Kunst	
107	**summer**	Sommer	
	fair	Jahrmarkt; *(hier:)* Schulfest	We can buy things at our school *fair*.
	sell	verkaufen	In a computer shop they *sell* computers.
	do sports	Sport(arten) treiben	I *do* lots of *sports*. I play football, I go jogging, I … .
	other	anderer/andere/anderes	
	partner	Partner/Partnerin	Has your school got a *partner* school in England?
	activity	Tätigkeit, Aktivität	
	band	Band, Gruppe	Terry plays the drums in the school *band*.
	winter	Winter	

Language

108	**discus**	Diskus	
	long jump	Weitsprung	
	race	Rennen	
	cricket	Kricket	
	take the times	die Zeiten messen	
	drink	trinken	
	sports field	Sportplatz	We can do sports in the sports hall or on the *sports field* outside.
	reporter	Reporter/Reporterin	
109	short	kurz	
	run from	weglaufen vor	
	volleyball	Volleyball	
	golf	Golf	
110	**usually**	normalerweise, gewöhnlich	Today, Mark is playing golf. He *usually* plays football.
	money	Geld	⚠ *Money* reimt sich mit dem Wort 'funny'.
	to	*(hier:)* um zu	
	stall	Bude, Stand	There are many *stalls* at the market.
	try	versuchen, ausprobieren	Can you play cricket? – No, but I can *try*.
	face painting	Kinderschminken	I like face *painting*. 

Sports

You do sports.	You play cricket.
… the long jump.	… football.
	… tennis.
You run in a race.	You go jogging.

110	**fire engine**	Feuerwehrauto	
	win	gewinnen	
	prize	Preis, Gewinn	You can *win* a race, a game, a *prize*.
	fresh	frisch	The milk from the farm is really *fresh*.
	sponge	Schwamm	
	jigsaw puzzle	Puzzle	Can you do *jigsaw puzzles*?
	you	euch	
111	**end**	Ende, Schluss	December is at the *end* of the year.
	ticket	Eintrittskarte, Ticket	

Text: Trouble at the disco

112	**trouble**	Schwierigkeiten, Ärger	*trouble* = problems
	only	nur	
	stand	stehen	sit, *stand*
	Leave me alone.	Lass mich in Ruhe.	What's wrong? – *Leave me alone*.
	open	offen, geöffnet	Many shops aren't *open* on Sunday.
	climb	klettern	⚠ Das 'b' wird nicht ausgesprochen.
113	**quick**	schnell	Sara often wins races. She's very *quick*.
	wait	warten	*Wait* for me!
	all evening	den ganzen Abend lang	Don't watch TV *all evening*.
	argue	diskutieren, streiten	Brothers and sisters often *argue*. ⚠ Der Teil 'gue' reimt sich mit dem Wort 'you'.
	boyfriend	Freund	Tim is Anna's *boyfriend*.
	lego	Lego	
	fight	kämpfen, sich prügeln	
	What's happening?	Was geht hier vor?	
	toilet	Toilette	

Practice

114	**teach**	unterrichten	Our sports teacher *teaches* hockey and volleyball.
	page	Seite	
115	**result**	Ergebnis, Resultat	Look, I've got the football *results*. Liverpool 2 – Arsenal 0
	competition	Wettbewerb, Wettkampf, Turnier	
	Wimbledon	*Tennisturnier, das jedes Jahr in London stattfindet*	
	star	Star, Stern	

Words

116	**chocolate**	Schokolade	
	month	Monat	There are twelve *months* in the year.

Lerncheck Unit 7

Kannst du Mini-Dialoge zusammenstellen? Eine Frage aus A passt zu einer Antwort aus B.

A	B
Anything else?	Two children are fighting.
What would you like to do?	No, thanks.
What's wrong with you?	I'd like to buy an ice cream.
What's happening?	Leave me alone!

In dieser alphabetischen Liste ist das gesamte Vokabular von *Let's go 1* enthalten. Namen werden in einer gesonderten Liste am Ende des Vokabulars aufgelistet.
Das Zeichen ⟨ ⟩ bei einer Angabe weist darauf hin, dass das Wort zum rezeptiven Wortschatz zählt.
Wendungen, die aus mehreren Wörtern bestehen, werden meist unter mehreren Stichwörten aufgeführt.
So ist z. B. *at home* unter *at* und *home* zu finden.
Die Zahlen verweisen auf das erstmalige Vorkommen der Wörter, z. B.
always U3, 46 = Unit 3, Seite 46
and LS, 8 = Let's start, Seite 8
animal B2, 42 = Bridge 2, Seite 42

A

a [ə] ein/eine **LS,** 8
about [ə'baʊt] über **U3,** 47
act [ækt] spielen *(eine Rolle)* **U7,** 106
activity [æk'tɪvəti] Tätigkeit, Aktivität **U7,** 107
activity centre [æk'tɪvəti 'sentə] Freizeitzentrum **U6,** 92
⟨add⟩ [æd] addiere/addiert **U3,** 57
⟨adventure⟩ [əd'ventʃə] Abenteuer **U6,** 98
after ['ɑ:ftə] nach **U2,** 30
... is after you [ɪz 'ɑ:ftə 'ju:] ... verfolgt dich, ... ist hinter dir her **LS,** 11
again [ə'gen] wieder **U2,** 34
all [ɔ:l] alle, alles **U1,** 18
all evening [ɔ:l 'i:vnɪŋ] den ganzen Abend lang **U7,** 113
alone [ə'ləʊn] alleine **U6,** 92
Leave me alone. [li:v mɪ: ə'ləʊn] Lass mich in Ruhe. **U7,** 112
along [ə'lɒŋ] entlang **U4,** 62
alphabet ['ælfəbet] Alphabet **U1,** 18
also ['ɔ:lsəʊ] auch **U5,** 80
always ['ɔ:lweɪz] immer **U3,** 46
an [ən] ein/eine **U1,** 17
and [ænd] und **LS,** 8
angry ['æŋgri] zornig, wütend **U2,** 34
animal ['ænɪml] Tier **B2,** 42
answer ['ɑ:nsə] beantworten, antworten **U4,** 66; Antwort **U4,** 65; ⟨**U3,** 57⟩
Anything else? [eniθɪŋ 'els] Sonst noch etwas? **U5,** 78
apple ['æpl] Apfel **U2,** 39
April ['eɪprl] April **U5,** 76
are [ɑ:] bist **LS,** 11; sind, seid **U1,** 13
argue ['ɑ:gju:] diskutieren, streiten **U7,** 113
art [ɑ:t] Kunst **U7,** 106
ask [ɑ:sk] fragen **U3,** 48
⟨asked⟩ [ɑ:skt] bat **U5,** 89
at [æt] in, auf, an, bei **U1,** 13; um **U4,** 66
at home [æt 'həʊm] zu Hause; daheim **U2,** 28
at the weekend [æt ðe wi:k'end] am Wochenende **U3,** 45
attic ['ætɪk] Dachboden, Speicher **U5,** 83
August ['ɔ:gəst] August **U5,** 76
autumn ['ɔ:təm] Herbst **U7,** 106
away [ə'weɪ] weg **U6,** 98; ⟨**U1,** 25⟩
awful ['ɔ:fl] furchtbar, scheußlich **U2,** 33

B

back [bæk] zurück **U5,** 82
bag [bæg] Tasche **U1,** 15
ball [bɔ:l] Ball **U1,** 18
balloon [bə'lu:n] Luftballon **U3,** 49
band [bænd] Band, Gruppe **U7,** 107
bark [bɑ:k] bellen **U3,** 51
basketball ['bɑ:skɪtbɔ:l] Basketball **B2,** 42
bathroom ['bɑ:θru:m] Badezimmer **B1,** 26
be [bi:] sein **U2,** 35
Be quiet. [bi: 'kwaɪət] Sei leise./Seid leise. **U2,** 35
beach [bi:tʃ] Strand **U6,** 92
⟨bear⟩ [beə] Bär **U7,** 119
because [bɪ'kɒz] weil **U5,** 82; ⟨**U1,** 25⟩
bed [bed] Bett **B1,** 26
go to bed [gəʊ tə 'bed] Schlafen gehen, ins Bett gehen **U3,** 51
bedroom ['bedru:m] Schlafzimmer **B1,** 26
behind [bɪ'haɪnd] hinter **U6,** 95
big [bɪg] groß **LS,** 11
bike [baɪk] Fahrrad **U4,** 69; ⟨**U2,** 41⟩
⟨bingo⟩ ['bɪngəʊ] Bingospiel **U3,** 49
bird [bɜ:d] Vogel **B2,** 42
birthday ['bɜ:θdeɪ] Geburtstag **U5,** 76
Happy birthday! ['hæpi 'bɜ:θdeɪ] Herzlichen Glückwunsch zum Geburtstag! **U5,** 76
blue [blu:] blau **LS,** 11
board [bɔ:d] Tafel, Anschlagtafel **U1,** 16
boat [bəʊt] Boot, Schiff **U4,** 60
book [bʊk] Buch, Heft **U1,** 15
boring ['bɔ:rɪŋ] langweilig **U1,** 18
box [bɒks] Kiste, Schachtel **U6,** 98
boy [bɔɪ] Junge **LS,** 10
boy band ['bɔɪ bænd] Boy Group **U3,** 45
boyfriend ['bɔɪfrend] Freund **U7,** 113
breakfast ['brekfəst] Frühstück **U2,** 33
have breakfast [hæv 'brekfəst] frühstücken **U3,** 50
break-in ['breɪkɪn] Einbruch **U6,** 99
⟨bridge⟩ [brɪdʒ] Brücke **B1,** 26
⟨bring⟩ [brɪŋ] bringe/bringt **U2,** 41
broken ['brəʊkn] kaputt **U1,** 15
brother ['brʌðə] Bruder **U2,** 29
brown [braʊn] braun **LS,** 11
bull [bʊl] Stier, Bulle **U6,** 95
bus [bʌs] Bus **U4,** 60
by (bus) [baɪ 'bʌs] mit (dem Bus) **U4,** 60
bush [bʊʃ] Busch, Gebüsch **U6,** 98
busy ['bɪzi] beschäftigt **U5,** 78
but [bʌt] aber **U1,** 14
butter ['bʌtə] Butter **U2,** 33
buy [baɪ] kaufen **U3,** 47
by [baɪ] von **U5,** 78
by (bus) [baɪ 'bʌs] mit (dem Bus) **U4,** 60

C

café [ˈkæfeɪ] Café **B3,** 58
cafeteria [kæfəˈtɪərɪə] Cafeteria **U1,** 17
cake [keɪk] Kuchen **U5,** 77
call [kɔːl] rufen, anrufen **U3,** 50
caller [ˈkɔːlə] Anrufer/Anruferin **U3,** 48
⟨camping trip⟩ [ˈkæmpɪŋ trɪp] Campingausflug **U6,** 105
can [kæn] können **U2,** 32; ⟨**U1,** 25⟩
can't [kɑːnt] nicht können **U2,** 33; ⟨**U1,** 25⟩
car [kɑː] Auto **U2,** 29
car park [ˈkɑː pɑːk] Parkplatz **B3,** 58
card [kɑːd] Karte **U5,** 77; Karte, Namensschild ⟨**LS,** 9⟩
card trick [ˈkɑːd trɪk] Kartentrick **U3,** 45
careful [ˈkeəfl] vorsichtig **U6,** 94
caretaker [ˈkeəteɪkə] Hausmeister/Hausmeisterin **U1,** 12
carry [ˈkæri] tragen **U6,** 98
cartoon [kɑːˈtuːn] Cartoon, Zeichentrickfilm **U2,** 32
cat [kæt] Katze **B1,** 26
CD [siːˈdiː] CD **U2,** 32
chair [tʃeə] Stuhl **U1,** 14
⟨chase⟩ [tʃeɪs] verfolgen, jagen **U7,** 119
chatterbox [ˈtʃætəbɒks] Plappermaul **LS,** 10
⟨check⟩ [tʃek] prüfen, kontrollieren **U1,** 25
⟨checklist⟩ [ˈtʃeklɪst] Checkliste, Kontrollliste **U1,** 25
⟨checkout⟩ [ˈtʃekaʊt] Abschlusskontrolle, Auschecken **U1,** 25
cheese [tʃiːz] Käse **B1,** 26
children *(pl.)* [ˈtʃɪldrn] Kinder **U3,** 50
chocolate [ˈtʃɒklət] Schokolade **U7,** 116; ⟨**U2,** 41⟩
church [tʃɜːtʃ] Kirche **U4,** 68
cinema [ˈsɪnəmə] Kino **U5,** 85
⟨class⟩ [klɑːs] Schulklasse, Klasse **U2,** 30
classroom [ˈklɑːsruːm] Klassenzimmer **U1,** 12
clever [ˈklevə] klug **U4,** 66
climb [klaɪm] klettern **U7,** 112
clock [klɒk] Uhr **B3,** 58
… o'clock [əˈklɒk] … Uhr **B3,** 58
close [kləʊz] schließen **U4,** 66
clothes [kləʊðz] Kleider, Kleidung **B4,** 74
cloudy [ˈklaʊdi] bewölkt, wolkig **B5,** 90
clown [klaʊn] Clown **B4,** 74
coffee [ˈkɒfi] Kaffee **U2,** 33
have a coffee [hæv ə ˈkɒfi] Kaffee trinken **U5,** 84
cold [kəʊld] kalt **U5,** 82
What **colour** is …? [wɒt ˈkʌlər ɪz] Welche Farbe hat …? **LS,** 11
come [kʌm] kommen **U4,** 64
Come on! [kʌm ˈɒn] Komm!/Kommt! **U5,** 82
comic [ˈkɒmɪk] Comicheft **U2,** 31
competition [kɒmpəˈtɪʃn] Wettbewerb, Wettkampf, Turnier **U7,** 115
computer [kəmˈpjuːtə] Computer **LS,** 8
cool [kuːl] prima, cool **LS,** 10
cornflakes [ˈkɔːnfleɪks] Cornflakes **U2,** 33
cousin [ˈkʌzn] Cousin/Cousine, Vetter **U3,** 46
cow [kaʊ] Kuh **B5,** 90
crazy [ˈkreɪzi] verrückt **U2,** 31
cricket [ˈkrɪkɪt] Kricket **U7,** 108
criminal [ˈkrɪmɪnl] Verbrecher/Verbrecherin **U6,** 98
cupboard [ˈkʌbəd] Küchenschrank, Schrank **B1,** 26

D

dad [dæd] Papa **U5,** 76
dance [dɑːns] tanzen **U3,** 45
dangerous [ˈdeɪndʒrəs] gefährlich **U6,** 94
⟨date⟩ [deɪt] Datum **U5,** 76
day [deɪ] Tag **U3,** 46
Dear [dɪə] Lieber/Liebe/Liebes *(in Briefanrede)* **U5,** 76
December [dɪˈsembə] Dezember **U5,** 76
⟨deck⟩ [dek] Deck **U4,** 73
design [dɪˈzaɪn] Muster, Entwurf **U5,** 83
⟨dialogue⟩ [ˈdaɪəlɒg] Dialog, Gespräch **U1,** 14
different [ˈdɪfrnt] verschieden, anders **U7,** 106
dining room [ˈdaɪnɪŋ ruːm] Esszimmer **B1,** 26
dinner [ˈdɪnə] Abendessen **U5,** 81
have dinner [hæv ˈdɪnə] zu Abend essen **U5,** 81
disco [ˈdɪskəʊ] Disko **U7,** 106
discus [ˈdɪskəs] Diskus **U7,** 108
⟨divide by⟩ [dɪˈvaɪd baɪ] dividiere durch/dividiert durch **U3,** 57
DJ [diːˈdʒeɪ] Diskjockey **U3,** 48
do [duː] tun, machen **U2,** 32
do sports [duː ˈspɔːts] Sport(arten) treiben **U7,** 107
dog [dɒg] Hund **U2,** 29
dog-tired [dɒgˈtaɪəd] hundemüde **U3,** 51
door [dɔː] Tür **U5,** 83
draw [drɔː] zeichnen **U2,** 37
drink [drɪŋk] Getränk **U5,** 78; ⟨**U2,** 41⟩; trinken **U7,** 108
⟨drink can⟩ [ˈdrɪŋk kæn] Getränkedose **U2,** 41
drive [draɪv] fahren **U6,** 98
driver [ˈdraɪvə] Fahrer/Fahrerin **U5,** 81
drums [drʌmz] Schlagzeug **U2,** 32
duck [dʌk] Ente **B5,** 90
DVD [diːviːˈdiː] DVD **U5,** 82
DVD player [diːviːˈdiː pleɪə] DVD-Spieler **U6,** 98

E

east [iːst] Osten **U4,** 60
easy [ˈiːzi] einfach **U1,** 18
eat [iːt] essen, fressen **U6,** 95
egg [eg] Ei **U2,** 33
eleven [ɪˈlevn] elf **LS,** 9
Anything **else?** [eniθɪŋ ˈels] Sonst noch etwas? **U5,** 78
e-mail [ˈiːmeɪl] E-Mail **U1,** 17
end [end] Ende, Schluss **U7,** 111
English [ˈɪŋglɪʃ] Engländer/Engländerin **U2,** 32
⟨in English⟩ [ɪn ˈɪŋglɪʃ] auf Englisch **U2,** 38
evening [ˈiːvnɪŋ] Abend **U3,** 50
all evening [ɔːl ˈiːvnɪŋ] den ganzen Abend lang **U7,** 113
in the evening [ɪn ðiː ˈiːvnɪŋ] am Abend; abends **U3,** 51
event [ɪˈvent] Ereignis, Veranstaltung **U7,** 106
every [ˈevri] jeder/jede/jedes **U3,** 46
everybody [ˈevribɒdi] jeder **U1,** 12
exchange [ɪksˈtʃeɪndʒ] Austausch **U7,** 106
Excuse me. [ɪkˈskjuːz mi] Entschuldigung. **U4,** 62
exercise book [ˈeksəsaɪz bʊk] Übungsheft **U1,** 15
expensive [ɪkˈspensɪv] teuer **U5,** 79

F

face [feɪs] Gesicht **U3,** 50
face painting ['feɪs peɪntɪŋ] Kinderschminken **U7,** 110
fair [feə] Jahrmarkt, Schulfest **U7,** 107
family ['fæmli] Familie **U2,** 28
famous ['feɪməs] berühmt **U4,** 61
fan [fæn] Fan **LS,** 8
fantastic [fæn'tæstik] fantastisch, toll **U5,** 83
farm [fɑ:m] Bauernhof **B5,** 90
farm machine ['fɑ:m məʃi:n] landwirtschaftliche Maschine **U6,** 95
⟨as fast as⟩ [əz 'fɑ:st əz] so schnell wie **U7,** 119
⟨faster⟩ ['fɑ:stə] schneller **U7,** 119
⟨faster than⟩ ['fɑ:stə ðæn] schneller als **U7,** 119
⟨the fastest⟩ [ðə 'fɑ:stɪst] der, die, das schnellste **U4,** 73
father ['fɑ:ðə] Vater **U2,** 28
favourite ['feɪvrɪt] Lieblings- **B2,** 42
February ['februri] Februar **U5,** 76
feed [fi:d] füttern **U6,** 94
felt-tip [felt'tɪp] Filzstift **U1,** 15
festival ['festɪvl] Fest **U7,** 106
fetch [fetʃ] holen, abholen **U5,** 80
field [fi:ld] Feld, Acker **B5,** 90
fight [faɪt] kämpfen, sich prügeln **U7,** 113
film [fɪlm] Film **U5,** 85
find [faɪnd] finden **U1,** 15
find out [faɪnd 'aʊt] herausfinden **U4,** 66
fine [faɪn] in Ordnung **U5,** 81
Fine, thanks. ['faɪn θæŋks] Danke, gut. **U1,** 13
finish ['fɪnɪʃ] beenden **U5,** 81
fire engine ['faɪə endʒɪn] Feuerwehrauto **U7,** 110
⟨first⟩ [fɜ:st] zum ersten Mal **U4,** 73
fish pl. **fish** [fɪʃ] Fisch **B2,** 42
flat [flæt] Wohnung **U2,** 28
follow ['fɒləʊ] folgen **U6,** 98
food [fu:d] Nahrung, Essen **B4,** 74
football ['fʊtbɔ:l] Fußball **U2,** 37
for [fɔ:] für **U2,** 28; ⟨**U1,** 22⟩
⟨forest⟩ ['fɒrɪst] Wald **U7,** 119
fresh [freʃ] frisch **U7,** 110
Friday ['fraɪdeɪ] Freitag **U2,** 30
friend [frend] Freund/Freundin **LS,** 10
frog [frɒg] Frosch **B2,** 42
from [frɒm] aus, von **LS,** 9
from … to [frɒm tʊ] von … bis **U3,** 46
I'm from … . ['aɪm frɒm] Ich komme aus … . **LS,** 9
Where are you from? [weər ɑ: jə 'frɒm] Woher kommst du? **LS,** 9
is/are **fun** [fʌn] macht/machen Spaß **U2,** 32
funny ['fʌni] komisch, lustig **U5,** 84
⟨further⟩ ['fɜ:ðə] weiter **U1,** 25

G

galaxy ['gæləksi] Galaxie, Milchstraße **U3,** 46
game [geɪm] Spiel **B1,** 26; ⟨**LS,** 11⟩
garden ['gɑ:dn] Garten **U2,** 28
⟨gave⟩ [geɪv] gab **U5,** 89
German ['dʒɜ:mən] Deutsch **U4,** 64
get [get] bekommen, kriegen **U5,** 77
get lost [get 'lɒst] sich verlaufen **U3,** 50
get up [get 'ʌp] aufstehen **U3,** 50
girl [gɜ:l] Mädchen **LS,** 8
give [gɪv] geben, schenken **U2,** 33
glass [glɑ:s] Glas **U5,** 78
glasses ['glɑ:sɪz] Brille **U5,** 85
go [gəʊ] gehen, fahren **U3,** 47
go jogging [gəʊ 'dʒɒgɪŋ] joggen gehen **U3,** 44
go on [gəʊ 'ɒn] weitermachen, weitergehen **U2,** 35
go out [gəʊ 'aʊt] ausgehen, ausfahren **U3,** 51
⟨go shopping⟩ [gəʊ 'ʃɒpɪŋ] einkaufen gehen **U5,** 81
go swimming [gəʊ 'swɪmɪŋ] schwimmen gehen **U3,** 44
go to bed [gəʊ tə 'bed] schlafen gehen, ins Bett gehen **U3,** 51
golf [gɒlf] Golf **U7,** 109
good [gʊd] gut **U1,** 18
good at ['gʊd æt] gut in **U1,** 18
Good morning. [gʊd 'mɔ:nɪŋ] Guten Morgen. **U1,** 12
Goodbye. [gʊd'baɪ] Auf Wiedersehen. **U1,** 18
⟨got⟩ [gɒt] erhielt **U5,** 89
⟨grammar⟩ ['græmə] Grammatik **U1,** 24
grandma ['grænmɑ:] Oma **U2,** 29
great [greɪt] großartig **U2,** 31
green [gri:n] grün **LS,** 11
group [gru:p] Gruppe **U1,** 14
guinea pig ['gɪni pɪg] Meerschweinchen **B2,** 42
guitar [gɪ'tɑ:] Gitarre **B2,** 42

H

⟨had⟩ [hæd] hatte **U5,** 89
half past [hɑ:f 'pɑ:st] halb **B3,** 58
hamburger ['hæmbɜ:gə] Hamburger **U6,** 96
What's **happening?** [wɒts 'hæpenɪŋ] Was geht hier vor? **U7,** 113
happy ['hæpi] glücklich, froh **U2,** 34
Happy birthday! ['hæpi 'bɜ:θdeɪ] Herzlichen Glückwunsch zum Geburtstag! **U5,** 76
hard [hɑ:d] schwierig, hart **U4,** 67
hat [hæt] Hut **B4,** 74
hate [heɪt] hassen, nicht mögen **U5,** 83
⟨have⟩ [hæv] haben **U5,** 89
⟨have to⟩ ['hæv tʊ] müssen **U7,** 119
⟨will have⟩ [wɪl 'hæv] werden haben **U6,** 105
⟨has stolen⟩ [hæs 'stəʊlən] hat gestohlen **U6,** 105
have a coffee [hæv ə 'kɒfi] Kaffee trinken **U5,** 84
have breakfast [hæv 'brekfəst] frühstücken **U3,** 50
have dinner [hæv 'dɪnə] zu Abend essen **U5,** 81
have lunch [hæv 'lʌnʃ] zu Mittag essen **U4,** 69
have got [hæv 'gɒt] haben, besitzen **U1,** 15
he [hi:] er **LS,** 10
hear [hɪə] hören **U4,** 64
⟨heavy⟩ ['hevɪ] schwer **U7,** 119
Hello. [hel'əʊ] Hallo. **LS,** 8
help [help] helfen **U2,** 34
hen [hen] Henne, Huhn **B5,** 90
her [hɜ:] ihr/ihre **U2,** 31; ihr; sie **U5,** 80
here [hɪə] hier **U1,** 12
Here you are. [hɪə ju: 'ɑ:] Hier bitte. **U1,** 19

Hi. [haɪ] Hallo. **U3**, 48
⟨hiker⟩ ['haɪkə] Wanderer/Wandrerin **U7**, 119
⟨hiking boots⟩ ['haɪkɪŋ bu:ts] Wanderschuhe **U7**, 119
him [hɪm] ihm; ihn **U3**, 47
his [hɪz] sein/seine **B1**, 26
hobby ['hɒbi] Hobby **U3**, 54; ⟨**B2**, 42⟩
hockey ['hɒki] Hockey **U3**, 53
holiday ['hɒlədeɪ] Ferien, Urlaub **U6**, 92
home [həʊm] Heim, Zuhause **U4**, 60; nach Hause **U3**, 50
at home [æt 'həʊm] zu Hause; daheim **U2**, 28
homework ['həʊmwɜ:k] Hausaufgaben **U2**, 34
hope [həʊp] hoffen **U6**, 96
hot [hɒt] heiß **U5**, 82
hotel [həʊ'tel] Hotel **U6**, 93; ⟨**U5**, 89⟩
house [haʊs] Haus **B1**, 26
how [haʊ] wie **U4**, 64
How are you? [haʊ 'ɑ: ju:] Wie geht's? **U1**, 13
⟨how many⟩ [haʊ 'meni] wie viele **U2**, 39
How much are they? [haʊ 'mʌtʃ ɑ: ðeɪ] Wie viel kosten sie? **U5**, 79
How much is it? [haʊ 'mʌtʃ ɪz ɪt] Wie viel kostet es? **U5**, 81
How old are you? [haʊ 'əʊld ɑ: ju:] Wie alt bist du? **LS**, 9

I

I [aɪ] ich **LS**, 8
I'd like to .... [aɪd 'laɪk tʊ] Ich würde gerne ...., Ich möchte **U5**, 77
I'm .... [aɪm] Ich bin .... **LS**, 8
I'm from .... ['aɪm frɒm] Ich komme aus .... **LS**, 9
I'm sorry. [aɪm 'sɒri] Tut mir Leid. **U1**, 19
ice cream ['aɪs kri:m] Eis, Eiscreme **U5**, 77
idea [aɪ'dɪə] Idee **U2**, 35
in [ɪn] in, im **LS**, 8
⟨in here⟩ [ɪn 'hɪə] hier hinein **U2**, 41
⟨in English⟩ [ɪn 'ɪŋglɪʃ] auf Englisch **U2**, 38
in front of [ɪn 'frʌnt əf] vor **U3**, 51
in the evening [ɪn ði: 'i:vnɪŋ] am Abend; abends **U3**, 51
in there [ɪn 'ðeə] da drin, dort drin **U5**, 83
in town [ɪn 'taʊn] in der Stadt **B3**, 58
⟨in 1869⟩ [ɪn 'eɪti:nsɪksti'‿naɪn] im Jahr 1869 **U4**, 73
in the morning [ɪn ðe 'mɔ:nɪŋ] am Morgen; morgens **U3**, 50
information [ɪnfə'meɪʃn] Information **U4**, 66
Information Centre [ɪnfə'meɪʃn sentə] Informationszentrum **U4**, 62
in-line skates ['ɪnlaɪn skeɪts] Inline-Skates, Inliner **U5**, 78
interesting ['ɪntrəstɪŋ] interessant **U4**, 60
into ['ɪntə] in, hinein **U4**, 62
⟨intro⟩ ['ɪntrəʊ] Einleitung **U1**, 12
⟨invitation⟩ [ɪnvɪ'teɪʃn] Einladung **U5**, 76
is [ɪz] ist **LS**, 8
How much is it? [haʊ 'mʌtʃ ɪz ɪt] Wie viel kostet es? **U5**, 81
... is after you [ɪz 'ɑ:ftə 'ju:] ... verfolgt dich, ... ist hinter dir her **LS**, 11
it [ɪt] es **LS**, 11
It's .... [ɪts] Es kostet **U5**, 81

J

January ['dʒænjʊri] Januar **U5**, 76
jigsaw puzzle ['dʒɪgsɔ: pʌzl] Puzzle **U7**, 110
job [dʒɒb] Arbeit, Beruf **U3**, 50
go **jogging** [gəʊ 'dʒɒgɪŋ] joggen gehen **U3**, 44
joke [dʒəʊk] Witz **U1**, 18
journalist ['dʒɜ:nlɪst] Journalist/Journalistin **U5**, 81
July [dʒʊ'laɪ] Juli **U5**, 76
June [dʒu:n] Juni **U5**, 76
⟨just⟩ [dʒʌst] nur **U7**, 119

K

karaoke [kæri'əʊki] Karaoke **U3**, 45
⟨kiosk⟩ ['ki:ɒsk] Kiosk **U2**, 41
kitchen ['kɪtʃɪn] Küche **B1**, 26
knife pl. **knives** [naɪf] Messer **U6**, 97
know [nəʊ] kennen, wissen **U4**, 64

L

⟨language⟩ ['læŋgwɪdʒ] Sprache **U1**, 14
lantern ['læntən] Laterne **U7**, 106
large [lɑ:dʒ] groß, riesig **U6**, 98
⟨last⟩ [lɑ:st] letzter/letzte/letztes **U3**, 55
⟨later⟩ ['leɪtə] später **U4**, 73
lazy ['leɪzi] faul **U4**, 66
leave [li:v] verlassen **U6**, 94
Leave me alone. [li:v mɪ: ə'ləʊn] Lass mich in Ruhe. **U7**, 112
left [left] links **U4**, 60
on the left [ɒn ðə 'left] links **U4**, 62
lego ['legəʊ] Lego **U7**, 113
let's [lets] lass/lasst uns **U1**, 15; ⟨**LS**, 9⟩
⟨let's start⟩ [lets 'stɑ:t] los geht's **LS**
letter ['letə] Buchstabe **U1**, 18
library ['laɪbrəri] Bücherei, Bibliothek **U1**, 17
like [laɪk] mögen, gern haben **U3**, 45
I'd like to .... [aɪd 'laɪk tʊ] Ich würde gerne ...., Ich möchte **U5**, 77
Would you like ...? [wʊd jə 'laɪk] Möchtest du ... ?/ Möchten Sie ... ? **U5**, 78
⟨list⟩ [lɪst] Liste **U1**, 22
listen ['lɪsn] zuhören, anhören **U1**, 18
listen to ['lɪsn tʊ] hören, anhören **U2**, 32
⟨listening⟩ ['lɪsnɪŋ] Hören; Hörübung **LS**, 9
live [lɪv] wohnen, leben **U4**, 66
living room ['lɪvɪŋ ru:m] Wohnzimmer **B1**, 26
long [lɒŋ] lang **U3**, 51
long jump ['lɒŋ dʒʌmp] Weitsprung **U7**, 108
look [lʊk] sehen, schauen **U4**, 60
⟨look up⟩ [lʊk 'ʌp] hinaufschauen **U6**, 105
look at ['lʊk æt] anschauen, ansehen **U4**, 63
look for ['lʊk fɔ:] suchen **U5**, 82
lots of ['lɒts əf] viele **U4**, 61
⟨loud⟩ [laʊd] laut **U2**, 41
love [lʌv] lieben, gern mögen **U5**, 80
be **lucky** ['lʌki] Glück haben **U2**, 34

lunch [lʌnʃ] Mittagessen **U1,** 18
have lunch [hæv 'lʌnʃ] zu Mittag essen **U4,** 69
lunch break ['lʌnʃ breɪk] Mittagspause **U1,** 18

M

make [meɪk] machen, tun **U2,** 35; ⟨**LS,** 9⟩
make up [meɪk 'ʌp] erfinden, sich ausdenken **U4,** 66
man pl. **men** [mæn; men] Mann **U3,** 49
⟨manager⟩ ['mænɪdʒə] Manager/Managerin **U5,** 89
⟨how many⟩ [haʊ 'meni] wie viele **U2,** 39
map [mæp] Stadtplan, Landkarte **U4,** 62
March [mɑ:tʃ] März **U5,** 76
market ['mɑ:kɪt] Markt **B3,** 58
matchstick man ['mætʃstɪk mæn] Strichmännchen **U6,** 101
⟨matchstick people⟩ ['mætʃstɪk pi:pl] *(pl.)* Strichmännchen **U6,** 101
May [meɪ] Mai **U5,** 76
maybe ['meɪbi] vielleicht **U2,** 34
me [mi:] mir; mich **U2,** 33
meal [mi:l] Mahlzeit, Essen **U4,** 65
mean [mi:n] bedeuten, heißen **U4,** 65
meet [mi:t] treffen, sich treffen, kennen lernen **B3,** 59
Nice to meet you. [naɪs tʊ 'mi:t ju:] Schön dich kennen zu lernen. **LS,** 10
meeting place ['mi:tɪŋ pleɪs] Treffpunkt **U2,** 28
men [men] Männer **U6,** 95
milk [mɪlk] Milch **U2,** 33
⟨What's missing?⟩ [wɒts 'mɪsɪŋ] Was fehlt? **U1,** 14
mobile phone [məʊbaɪl 'fəʊn] Handy, Mobiltelefon **U4,** 71
modern ['mɒdn] modern **U1,** 17
Monday ['mʌndeɪ] Montag **U3,** 44
money ['mʌni] Geld **U7,** 110
monster ['mɒnstə] Monster, Ungeheuer **LS,** 11
month [mʌnθ] Monat **U7,** 116
⟨moon⟩ [mu:n] Mond **U1,** 25
morning ['mɔ:nɪŋ] Morgen, Vormittag **U3,** 50
in the morning [ɪn ðe 'mɔ:nɪŋ] am Morgen; morgens **U3,** 50
mother ['mʌðə] Mutter **U2,** 28
mouse [maʊs] Maus **LS,** 9
Mr ['mɪstə] *(Anrede)* Herr **U1,** 12
Mrs ['mɪsɪz] *(Anrede)* Frau **U1,** 12
much [mʌtʃ] viel **U5,** 78
How much are they? [haʊ 'mʌtʃ ɑ: ðeɪ] Wie viel kosten sie? **U5,** 79
How much is it? [haʊ 'mʌtʃ ɪz ɪt] Wie viel kostet es? **U5,** 81
⟨multiply by⟩ ['mʌltɪplaɪ baɪ] multipliziere mit/multipliziert mit **U3,** 57
mum [mʌm] Mama **U5,** 76
⟨museum⟩ [mju:'zi:əm] Museum **U4,** 73
music ['mju:zɪk] Musik **LS,** 10
must [mʌst] müssen **U6,** 94
my [maɪ] mein/meine **LS,** 9
My name is .... [maɪ 'neɪm ɪz] Ich heiße .... **LS,** 8

N

name [neɪm] Name **LS,** 8
⟨name card⟩ [neɪm 'kɑ:d] Namensschild **LS,** 9
My name is .... [maɪ 'neɪm ɪz] Ich heiße .... **LS,** 8
What's your name? [wɒts jɔ: 'neɪm] Wie heißt du? **LS,** 8
near [nɪə] nahe, in der Nähe von **U6,** 99
⟨nearer and nearer⟩ ['nɪərə ænd 'nɪərə] immer näher **U7,** 119
never ['nevə] nie, niemals **U3,** 46
new [nju:] neu **LS,** 8
next to ['neks tʊ] neben **B3,** 58
nice [naɪs] nett, schön **U2,** 31
Nice to meet you. [naɪs tʊ 'mi:t ju:] Schön dich kennen zu lernen. **LS,** 10
⟨night⟩ [naɪt] Nacht **U6,** 105
no [nəʊ] nein **U1,** 14; kein/keine ⟨**U2,** 41⟩
noise [nɔɪz] Geräusch, Lärm **U6,** 95
north [nɔ:θ] Norden **U4,** 60
not [nɒt] nicht **U1,** 14
November [nəʊ'vembə] November **U5,** 76
now [naʊ] jetzt, nun **U1,** 18
number ['nʌmbə] Nummer **LS,** 9
nurse [nɜ:s] Krankenpfleger/Krankenschwester **U2,** 32

O

October [ɒk'təʊbə] Oktober **U5,** 76
of [ɒv] von **U4,** 60
often ['ɒfn] oft **U3,** 46
oh [əʊ] null **LS,** 9
Oh. [əʊ] Oh. **U1,** 14
OK [əʊ'keɪ] OK, in Ordnung **U1,** 14
old [əʊld] alt **U1,** 13
How old are you? [haʊ 'əʊld ɑ: ju:] Wie alt bist du? **LS,** 9
on [ɒn] am, auf **U2,** 33
on Sunday [ɒn 'sʌndeɪ] am Sonntag; sonntags **U2,** 33
on the programme [ɒn ðə 'prəʊgræm] in der Sendung **U3,** 46
one [wʌn] eins **LS,** 9
only ['əʊnli] nur **U7,** 112; ⟨**U5,** 89⟩
open ['əʊpn] öffnen **U4,** 66; offen, geöffnet **U7,** 112
opposite ['ɒpəzɪt] gegenüber (von) **B3,** 58
or [ɔ:] oder **U2,** 28; ⟨**LS,** 10⟩
orange juice ['ɒrɪndʒ 'dʒu:s] Orangensaft **U5,** 78
⟨order⟩ ['ɔ:də] Reihenfolge **LS,** 9
other ['ʌðə] anderer/andere/anderes **U7,** 107
our ['aʊə] unser/unsere **U3,** 48
outside [aʊt'saɪd] außen, draußen, außerhalb **U1,** 18
over ['əʊvə] über **U2,** 28
own [əʊn] eigener/eigene/eigenes **U2,** 31

P

pair [peə] Paar **U3,** 54
⟨a pair of trainers⟩ [ə peə əv 'treɪnəz] ein Paar Turnschuhe **U7,** 119
⟨paper⟩ ['peɪpə] Zeitung **U2,** 41
parents ['peərənts] Eltern **U4,** 68
park [pɑ:k] Park **U3,** 49
part [pɑ:t] Teil **U4,** 60; ⟨**U3,** 44⟩
partner ['pɑ:tnə] Partner/Partnerin **U7,** 107; ⟨**U1,** 14⟩
party ['pɑ:ti] Party **U2,** 32
have a party [hæv ə 'pɑ:ti] eine Party feiern **U2,** 32

past [pɑːst] nach **B3,** 58
half past [hɑːf ˈpɑːst] halb **B3,** 58
quarter past [ˈkwɔːtə pɑːst] viertel nach **B3,** 58
path [pɑːθ] Pfad, Weg **U6,** 98
pen [pen] Füller **U1,** 15
pencil [ˈpentsl] Bleistift **U1,** 15
pencil case [ˈpentsl keɪs] Federmäppchen **U1,** 15
people [ˈpiːpl] Leute, Menschen **U3,** 46; ⟨**U2,** 35⟩
⟨person⟩ [ˈpɜːsn] Person **U5,** 89
pet [pet] Haustier **B2,** 43
phone [fəʊn] anrufen **U3,** 46
photo [ˈfəʊtəʊ] Foto, Fotografie **U5,** 85
picture [ˈpɪktʃə] Bild **U1,** 15
pig [pɪg] Schwein **U6,** 100
pink [pɪŋk] pink, rosa **LS,** 11
plan [plæn] Plan **U4,** 67
play [pleɪ] Spiel, Theaterstück **U7,** 106; spielen **U1,** 19
player [ˈpleɪə] Spieler/Spielerin **U3,** 53
please [pliːz] bitte **U1,** 19; ⟨**LS,** 9⟩
police pl. **police** [pəˈliːs] Polizei **U6,** 99
police officer [pəˈliːs ˈɒfɪsə] Polizist/Polizistin **U6,** 99
pond [pɒnd] Teich **B5,** 90
pony [ˈpəʊni] Pony **B5,** 90
pop star [ˈpɒp stɑː] Popstar **U3,** 46
poster [ˈpəʊstə] Poster **U2,** 38; ⟨**U1,** 21⟩
post office [ˈpəʊst ɒfɪs] Postamt **B3,** 58
pound [paʊnd] Pfund *(britische Währungseinheit)* **U5,** 79
⟨practice⟩ [ˈpræktɪs] Übung **U1,** 20
practise [ˈpræktɪs] üben **U3,** 45
present [ˈpreznt] Geschenk **U5,** 77
prize [praɪz] Preis, Gewinn **U7,** 110
problem [ˈprɒbləm] Problem **U1,** 18
procession [prəˈseʃn] Umzug, Festzug **U7,** 106
programme [ˈprəʊgræm] Sendung **U3,** 46
on the programme [ɒn ðə ˈprəʊgræm] in der Sendung **U3,** 46
project [ˈprɒdʒekt] Projekt **U4,** 64; ⟨**U1,** 21⟩
project day [ˈprɒdʒekt deɪ] Projekttag **U4,** 64
pupil [ˈpjuːpl] Schüler/Schülerin **U1,** 14
put [pʊt] setzen, stellen, legen **U6,** 98; hinein tun ⟨**U2,** 41⟩
⟨put on⟩ [pʊt ˈɒn] anziehen **U7,** 119

Q

quarter past [ˈkwɔːtə pɑːst] viertel nach **B3,** 58
question [ˈkwestʃən] Frage **U4,** 64; ⟨**U2,** 37⟩
quiet [ˈkwaɪət] leise **U2,** 35
Be quiet. [biː ˈkwaɪət] Sei/Seid leise. **U2,** 35
quiz [kwɪz] Quiz **U3,** 46

R

rabbit [ˈræbɪt] Kaninchen **B2,** 42
race [reɪs] Rennen **U7,** 108
radio [ˈreɪdiəʊ] Radio **U2,** 31
rainy [ˈreɪni] regnerisch, verregnet **B5,** 90
⟨rap⟩ [ræp] Rap **B1,** 27
read [riːd] lesen **U2,** 32
ready [ˈredi] fertig **U4,** 67
really [ˈrɪəli] wirklich **U5,** 80
red [red] rot **LS,** 11
repair [rɪˈpeə] reparieren **U6,** 95
reporter [rɪˈpɔːtə] Reporter/Reporterin **U7,** 108
restaurant [ˈrestrɑːŋ] Restaurant, Gaststätte **U4,** 66
result [rɪˈzʌlt] Ergebnis, Resultat **U7,** 115
right [raɪt] rechts **U4,** 60; richtig **U1,** 18; ⟨**LS,** 9⟩
on the right [ɒn ðə ˈraɪt] rechts **U4,** 62
river [ˈrɪvə] Fluss **U4,** 60
road [rəʊd] Straße **U3,** 51
robot [ˈrəʊbɒt] Roboter **B4,** 74
room [ruːm] Zimmer, Raum **U1,** 17
rubber [ˈrʌbə] Radiergummi **U1,** 15
⟨rubbish⟩ [ˈrʌbɪʃ] Abfall, Müll **U2,** 41
rucksack [ˈrʌksæk] Rucksack **B1,** 26
rule [ruːl] Regel **U2,** 35
ruler [ˈruːlə] Lineal **U1,** 15
run [rʌn] laufen, rennen **U6,** 95
run from [ˈrʌn frɒm] weglaufen vor **U7,** 109

S

sad [sæd] traurig, schmerzlich **U5,** 82
⟨sailed⟩ [seɪld] segelte **U4,** 73
⟨sailor⟩ [seɪlə] Seemann **U4,** 73
the **same** [seɪm] derselbe/dieselbe/dasselbe **U4,** 64
sandwich [ˈsænwɪdʒ] Sandwich, belegtes Brot **B4,** 74; ⟨**U2,** 41⟩
Saturday [ˈsætədeɪ] Samstag **U2,** 34
say [seɪ] sagen **B2,** 43
school [skuːl] Schule **U1,** 12
school team [skuːl ˈtiːm] Schulmannschaft **U3,** 44
⟨sea⟩ [siː] Meer **U4,** 73
see [siː] sehen **U3,** 53; ⟨**U1,** 25⟩
See you there. [siː jə ˈðeə] Wir sehen uns dort. **U3,** 53
sell [sel] verkaufen **U7,** 107
send [send] schicken, senden **U3,** 46
⟨sentence⟩ [ˈsentəns] Satz **U3,** 44
September [sepˈtembə] September **U5,** 76
she [ʃiː] sie **LS,** 10
shed [ʃed] Schuppen **U2,** 28
sheep pl. **sheep** [ʃiːp] Schaf **B5,** 90
shoe [ʃuː] Schuh **U3,** 51
shop [ʃɒp] Laden, Geschäft **LS,** 8
⟨go shopping⟩ [gəʊ ˈʃɒpɪŋ] einkaufen gehen **U5,** 81
⟨short⟩ [ʃɔːt] kurz **U7,** 109
show [ʃəʊ] zeigen **U6,** 99
⟨sign⟩ [saɪn] Schild, Zeichen **U4,** 70
sing [sɪŋ] singen **U3,** 45
⟨Sir⟩ [sɜː] Herr *(Anrede; Titel)* **U1,** 25
sister [ˈsɪstə] Schwester **U2,** 28
sit [sɪt] sitzen **U3,** 51
⟨sit down⟩ [sɪt ˈdaʊn] sich hinsetzen **U7,** 119
skateboard [ˈskeɪtbɔːd] Skateboard **U2,** 36
skirt [skɜːt] Rock **B4,** 74
⟨sky⟩ [skaɪ] Himmel **U6,** 105
sleep [sliːp] schlafen **U3,** 51
sleeping bag [ˈsliːpɪŋ bæg] Schlafsack **U6,** 97
small [smɔːl] klein **U2,** 31

snack [snæk] Imbiss, Snack **U5,** 84
so [səʊ] so **U4,** 66; also, folglich **U6,** 96
sofa ['səʊfə] Sofa **B1,** 26
some [sʌm] einige, etwas **U6,** 97
⟨somebody⟩ ['sʌmbədi] jemand **U6,** 105
sometimes ['sʌmtaɪmz] manchmal **U3,** 46
song [sɒŋ] Lied **U3,** 48
soon [su:n] bald **U5,** 78
I'm **sorry.** [aɪm 'sɒri] Tut mir Leid. **U1,** 19
south [saʊθ] Süden **U4,** 60
southwest [saʊθ'west] südwestlich, Südwest- **U6,** 92
speak [spi:k] sprechen **U4,** 64
⟨speaking⟩ ['spi:kɪŋ] Sprechen, Sprechübung **LS,** 10
special ['speʃl] besonderer, besondere, besonderes **U5,** 82
⟨spell⟩ [spel] buchstabiere/buchstabiert **U1,** 16
spider ['spaɪdə] Spinne **U5,** 83
sponge [spʌndʒ] Schwamm **U7,** 110
sports [spɔ:ts] Sport **U1,** 18
do sports [du: 'spɔ:ts] Sport (-arten) treiben **U7,** 107
sports field ['spɔ:ts fi:ld] Sportplatz **U7,** 108
sports hall ['spɔ:ts hɔ:l] Turnhalle **U1,** 17
spring [sprɪŋ] Frühling **U7,** 106
stall [stɔ:l] Bude, Stand **U7,** 110
stand [stænd] stehen **U7,** 112
star [stɑ:] Star, Stern **U7,** 115; ⟨**U1,** 16⟩
start [stɑ:t] anfangen **U3,** 48
⟨let's start⟩ [lets 'stɑ:t] los geht's **LS**
stay [steɪ] wohnen, übernachten **U6,** 92
still [stɪl] noch **U5,** 82
⟨stop⟩ [stɒp] anhalten, stoppen **U7,** 119
⟨story⟩ ['stɔ:ri] Geschichte **U3,** 50
straight on [streɪt 'ɒn] geradeaus **U4,** 62
street [stri:t] Straße **U4,** 62
stress [stres] Stress, Belastung **U5,** 78
stressed [strest] gestresst, belastet **U5,** 78
⟨suddenly⟩ ['sʌdnli] plötzlich **U7,** 119
summer ['sʌmə] Sommer **U7,** 107
Sunday ['sʌndeɪ] Sonntag **U2,** 33
on Sunday [ɒn 'sʌndeɪ] am Sonntag; sonntags **U2,** 33
sunny ['sʌni] sonnig, heiter **B5,** 90
sure [ʃɔ:] sicher **U4,** 65
survey ['sɜ:veɪ] Umfrage **U3,** 47
sweatshirt ['swetʃɜ:t] Sweatshirt **U4,** 71
go **swimming** [gəʊ 'swɪmɪŋ] schwimmen gehen **U3,** 44
swimming pool ['swɪmɪŋ pu:l] Schwimmbad **U4,** 68

T

table ['teɪbl] Tisch **U1,** 16
take [teɪk] nehmen, mitnehmen **U3,** 50; mit … fahren **U4,** 63
⟨take away⟩ [teɪk ə'weɪ] nehmen, mitnehmen **U3,** 57
⟨take off⟩ [teɪk 'ɒf] ausziehen **U7,** 119
take part in [teɪk 'pɑ:t ɪn] teilnehmen an **U7,** 106
take the times [teɪk ðə 'taɪmz] die Zeiten messen **U7,** 108
talk about [tɔ:k ə'baʊt] sprechen über, reden über **U2,** 34
talk to ['tɔ:k tʊ] sprechen mit, reden mit **U3,** 46
taxi ['tæksi] Taxi **U5,** 80
tea [ti:] Tee **U2,** 33
teach [ti:tʃ] unterrichten **U7,** 114
teacher ['ti:tʃə] Lehrer/Lehrerin **U1,** 12
team [ti:m] Mannschaft, Team **U3,** 53
telephone ['telɪfəʊn] Telefon **LS,** 9
television ['telɪvɪʒn] Fernseher **U6,** 96
tell [tel] sagen, erzählen **U6,** 94
tennis ['tenɪs] Tennis **B2,** 42
tent [tent] Zelt **U6,** 97
term [tɜ:m] Trimester, Semester **U7,** 106
text [tekst] Text **U1,** 17
thank you ['θæŋkju:] danke (schön) **U1,** 14
Fine, **thanks.** ['faɪn θæŋks] Danke, gut. **U1,** 13
that [ðæt] das; jener/jene/jenes **U1,** 12
That's that! [ðæts 'ðæt] Damit basta! **U2,** 34
the [ðə] der, die, das **U1,** 12; ⟨**LS,** 9⟩
the same [seɪm] derselbe/dieselbe/dasselbe **U4,** 64
their [ðeə] ihr/ihre **U3,** 48
them [ðem] sie; ihnen **U5,** 80
then [ðen] dann **U3,** 50; ⟨**U3,** 47⟩
there [ðeə] da, dort **U1,** 16
in there [ɪn 'ðeə] da drin, dort drin **U5,** 83
See you there. [si: jə 'ðeə] Wir sehen uns dort. **U3,** 53
there are [ðeə 'ɑ:] da sind **U3,** 49
there is [ðeə 'ɪz] da ist, es gibt, es ist **U3,** 49
these [ði:z] diese **U5,** 79
they [ðeɪ] *(pl.)* sie **U1,** 13
They're …. [ðeə] Sie kosten …. **U5,** 79
thing [θɪŋ] Ding, Sache **U2,** 31
think [θɪŋk] finden, meinen, denken **U3,** 52
⟨think of⟩ ['θɪŋk əf] Denk dir/Denkt euch **U3,** 57
thirsty ['θɜ:sti] durstig **U5,** 86
this [ðɪs] dieser/diese/dieses **LS,** 8
this is [ðɪs ɪz] dies ist, das ist **LS,** 8
this is why [ðɪs ɪz 'waɪ] deshalb **U5,** 83
those [ðəʊz] jene **U5,** 83
⟨thousands⟩ ['θaʊzəndz] tausende **U6,** 105
throw [θrəʊ] werfen **U3,** 51
Thursday ['θɜ:zdeɪ] Donnerstag **U3,** 44
ticket ['tɪkɪt] Eintrittskarte, Ticket **U7,** 111
tidy ['taɪdi] ordentlich, sauber **U2,** 31
time [taɪm] Zeit **B3,** 58
take the times [teɪk ðə 'taɪmz] die Zeiten messen **U7,** 108
What time ist it? [wɒt 'taɪm ɪz ɪt] Wie viel Uhr ist es? **B3,** 58
tired ['taɪəd] müde **U3,** 51
to [tʊ] an, nach, zu **U1,** 17; vor **B3,** 58; um zu **U7,** 110
toast [təʊst] Toast(brot) **U2,** 33
today [tə'deɪ] heute **U3,** 47
toilet ['tɔɪlət] Toilette **U7,** 113
tomorrow [tə'mɒrəʊ] morgen **U5,** 80
too [tu:] auch **LS,** 9; zu **U5,** 78
⟨took⟩ [tʊk] nahm, brachte **U4,** 73

torch [tɔːtʃ] Taschenlampe **U6,** 97
tourist ['tʊərɪst] Tourist/Touristin **U4,** 60
town [taʊn] Stadt **B3,** 58
in town [ɪn 'taʊn] in der Stadt **B3,** 58
tractor ['træktə] Traktor **B5,** 90
train [treɪn] Zug **U4,** 60; trainieren **U3,** 44
⟨a pair of trainers⟩ [ə peə əv 'treɪnəz] ein Paar Turnschuhe **U7,** 119
⟨training boat⟩ [treɪnɪŋ 'bəʊt] Schulschiff **U4,** 73
tree [triː] Baum **U2,** 28
trick [trɪk] Trick **U4,** 67; ⟨**U3,** 57⟩
trouble ['trʌbl] Schwierigkeiten, Ärger **U7,** 112
trousers ['traʊzez] Hose **B4,** 74
try [traɪ] versuchen, ausprobieren **U7,** 110
T-shirt ['tiːʃɜːt] T-Shirt **B4,** 74
Tuesday ['tjuːzdeɪ] Dienstag **U3,** 44
tunnel ['tʌnl] Tunnel, Unterführung **U4,** 60
turn [tɜːn] abbiegen **U4,** 62
tutor group ['tjuːtə gruːp] Klasse *(in einer englischen Schule)* **U1,** 14
TV [tiː'viː] Fernseher **B1,** 26
twenty-six [twenti 'sɪks] sechsundzwanzig **U1,** 18

U

under ['ʌndə] unter **U4,** 60
Underground ['ʌndəgraʊnd] U-Bahn **U4,** 60
uniform ['juːnɪfɔːm] Uniform **U1,** 12
⟨unit⟩ ['juːnɪt] Kapitel **U1,** 12
us [ʌs] uns; wir **U5,** 80
usually ['juːʒli] normalerweise, gewöhnlich **U7,** 110

V

van [væn] Lieferwagen, Kleintransporter **B1,** 27
vegetable ['vedʒtəbl] Gemüse **U6,** 96
very ['veri] sehr **U3,** 48
video camera ['vɪdiəʊ kæmrə] Videokamera, Camcorder **U6,** 98
visit ['vɪzɪt] Besuch **U7,** 106; besuchen **U6,** 92
volleyball ['vɒlibɔːl] Volleyball **U7,** 109

W

⟨wait⟩ [weɪt] warten **U5,** 89
walk [wɔːk] gehen, laufen **U4,** 60
want to ['wɒnt tʊ] wollen, mögen **U6,** 92
⟨wanted to⟩ ['wɒntɪd] wollten **U5,** 89
⟨was⟩ [wɒz] war **U4,** 72
wash [wɒʃ] waschen **U3,** 50
watch [wɒtʃ] anschauen, zusehen **U2,** 32; beobachten **U6,** 99
water ['wɔːtə] Wasser **U6,** 97
we [wiː] wir **U1,** 13
wear [weə] *(Kleidung)* anhaben, tragen **U6,** 100
weather ['weðə] Wetter **B5,** 90
Wednesday ['wenzdeɪ] Mittwoch **U3,** 44
week [wiːk] Woche **U4,** 63
weekend [wiːk'end] Wochenende **U3,** 45
at the weekend [æt ðe wiːk'end] am Wochenende **U3,** 45
You're **welcome.** [jɒː 'welkəm] Bitte / Gern geschehen. **U5,** 83
⟨welcome to …⟩ ['welkəm tʊ] willkommen in … **U2,** 41
⟨went⟩ [went] gingen **U5,** 89
west [west] Westen **U4,** 60
what [wɒt] was **LS,** 8; welcher/welche/welches **LS,** 11
What colour is …? [wɒt 'kʌlər ɪz] Welche Farbe hat …? **LS,** 11
What's happening? [wɒts 'hæpenɪŋ] Was geht hier vor? **U7,** 113
⟨What's missing?⟩ [wɒts 'mɪsɪŋ] Was fehlt? **U1,** 14
What's wrong? [wɒts 'rɒŋ] Was ist los? **U1,** 14
What's your name? [wɒts jɔː 'neɪm] Wie heißt du? **LS,** 8
What time ist it? [wɒt 'taɪm ɪz ɪt] Wie viel Uhr ist es? **B3,** 58
when [wen] wann **U4,** 66; ⟨**U3,** 51⟩
where [weə] wo **U1,** 14; wohin **U6,** 93
Where are you from? [weər ɑː jə 'frɒm] Woher kommst du? **LS,** 9
which [wɪtʃ] welcher/welche/welches **U5,** 83; ⟨**U1,** 25⟩
who [huː] wer **U1,** 15
why [waɪ] warum **U4,** 64; ⟨**U1,** 25⟩
this is why [ðɪs ɪz 'waɪ] deshalb **U5,** 83
wild [waɪld] wild **U6,** 92
win [wɪn] gewinnen **U7,** 110
window ['wɪndəʊ] Fenster **U1,** 16
winter ['wɪntə] Winter **U7,** 107
with [wɪð] mit, mit … zusammen, bei **U1,** 18; ⟨mit⟩ **U1,** 14
woman pl. **women** ['wʊmən; 'wɪmɪn] Frau **U6,** 95
⟨wool⟩ [wʊl] Wolle **U4,** 73
word [wɜːd] Wort **U1,** 18; ⟨**U1,** 13⟩
⟨word web⟩ [web] Wortnetz **U1,** 22
work [wɜːk] Arbeit **U5,** 81; arbeiten **U3,** 46; funktionieren **U4,** 65
worksheet ['wɜːkʃiːt] Arbeitsblatt **U4,** 64
be **worried** ['wʌrid] beunruhigt sein, besorgt sein **U2,** 35
I'd like to …. [aɪd 'laɪk tʊ] Ich würde gerne …., Ich möchte …. **U5,** 77
Would you like …? [wʊd jə 'laɪk] Möchtest du … ?/ Möchten Sie … ? **U5,** 78
write [raɪt] schreiben **U4,** 64
wrong [rɒŋ] falsch **U1,** 12
What's wrong? [wɒts 'rɒŋ] Was ist los? **U1,** 14

Y

year [jɪə] Jahr **U4,** 64
Year 7 [jiə 'sevn] Klasse sieben **U1,** 12
yellow ['jeləʊ] gelb **LS,** 11
yes [jes] ja **U1,** 13
you [juː] du **LS,** 9; *(pl.)* ihr **U1,** 13; dir; dich **U3,** 48; euch **U7,** 110; man ⟨**U1,** 25⟩
You're welcome. [jɒː 'welkəm] Bitte. / Gern geschehen. **U5,** 83
young [jʌŋ] jung **U3,** 46
your [jɔː] dein/deine **LS,** 9; euer/eure, Ihr/Ihre **U3,** 48

Boys' names

Andy ['ændi] **U7,** 115
Ben [ben] **U2,** 29
Dan [dæn] **U3,** 46
Luke [lu:k] **U7,** 111
Mark [mɑ:k] **B4,** 74
Matt [mæt] **U7,** 113
Richard ['rɪtʃəd] **U3,** 50
Sam [sæm] **LS,** 8
Scott [skɒt] **U7,** 115
Simon ['saɪmən] **U7,** 111
Steven ['sti:vn] **U7,** 115
Terry ['teri] **LS,** 8
Tim [tɪm] **B4,** 74
Tom [tɒm] **LS,** 9
⟨Tommy⟩ ['tɒmi] **U1,** 25

Girls' names

Anna ['ænə] **B4,** 74
Emma ['emə] **LS,** 8
Eva ['ɪ:və] **U6,** 102
Farah ['fɑ:rə] **U2,** 32
Helen ['helən] **U5,** 80
Jade [dʒeɪd] **U2,** 29
Jenny ['dʒeni] **U4,** 64
Katie ['keɪti] **U7,** 114
Linda ['lɪndə] **B4,** 74
Lisa ['li:sə] **LS,** 8
Nasreen [nʌs'ri:n] **U2,** 28
Nina ['ni:nə] **U2,** 28
Susan ['su:zn] **U3,** 50
Susie ['su:zi] **B1,** 27
Tara ['tɑ:rə] **U7,** 111

Surnames

Bray [breɪ] **U7,** 115
Brook [brʊk] **LS,** 9
Brown [braʊn] **U7,** 115
Carter ['kɑ:tə] **U1,** 12
Clark [klɑ:k] **U5,** 80
Harvey ['hɑ:vi] **U7,** 115
Hu [hu:] **U4,** 66
Jackson ['dʒæksən] **LS,** 10
Newman ['nju:mən] **U1,** 12
Penford ['penfɔ:d] **U7,** 112
Richards ['rɪtʃədz] **U6,** 95
Rose [rəʊz] **U4,** 66
Spencer ['spentsə] **LS,** 9
Taylor ['teɪlə] **LS,** 10
Webb [web] **U7,** 115
Williams ['wɪljəmz] **U7,** 115

Place names

⟨Australia⟩ [ɒs'treɪliə] **U1,** 25
Berlin [bɜ:'lɪn] **U7,** 106
⟨Brook Park⟩ [brʊk 'pɑ:k] **U2,** 41
⟨China⟩ ['tʃaɪnə] **U4,** 73
Crane Street ['kreɪn stri:t] **U4,** 62
Dartmoor ['dɑ:tmɔ:] **U6,** 92
Devon ['devn] **U6,** 92
⟨Earth⟩ [ɜ:θ] **U4,** 73
England ['ɪŋglənd] **U6,** 92; ⟨**U4,** 73⟩
Germany ['dʒɜ:məni] **U1,** 15
Greenwich ['grenɪdʒ] **LS,** 8
Greenwich Market [grenɪdʒ 'mɑ:kɪt] **U4,** 61
Greenwich Road [grenɪdʒ 'rəʊd] **U2,** 28
Hither Farm Road [hɪðə fɑ:m 'rəʊd] **U2,** 28
Holburn Road [hɒlbɜ:n 'rəʊd] **U2,** 32
India ['ɪndiə] **U2,** 32
King William Walk [kɪŋ wɪljəm 'wɒ:k] **U4,** 62
London ['lʌndən] **LS,** 8
London Road [lʌndən 'rəʊd] **B3,** 58
Nelson Road [nelsn 'rəʊd] **U4,** 62
New York [nju:'jɔ:k] **U4,** 65
Park Row [pɑ:k 'rəʊ] **U4,** 62
River Thames [rɪvə 'temz] **U4,** 60
Romney Road [rɒmni 'rəʊd] **U4,** 61
Wendover Road [wendəʊvə 'rəʊd] **U2,** 29

Other names

Barker ['bɑ:kə] **U2,** 29
Beatles ['bi:tlz] **U5,** 80
Blue Note Café [blu: nəʊt 'kæfeɪ] **U4,** 62
Brad Pitt [bræd 'pɪt] **U5,** 78
Bugsy Malone [bʌgzi mə'ləʊn] **U7,** 106
Burger Bar [bɜ:gə bɑ:] **U4,** 63
Cutty Sark [kʌti 'sɑ:k] **U4,** 60
David Bowie [deɪvɪd 'baʊi] **U5,** 80
Dartmoor Safaris [dɑ:tmɔ: sə'fɑ:riz] **U6,** 93
⟨Doctor Watson⟩ [dɒktə 'wɒtsn] **U6,** 105
Formula One [fɔ:mjələ 'wʌn] **U3,** 45
Galaxy Radio [gæləksi 'reɪdiəʊ] **U3,** 46
Garden Restaurant [gɑ:dn 'restərənt] **U4,** 62
Greendale Farm [gri:ndeɪl 'fɑ:m] **U6,** 94
Greenwich Mean Time [grenɪdʒ 'mi:n taɪm] **U4,** 65
Meridian Line [mə'rɪdiən laɪn] **U4,** 60
Mr Bean [mɪstə 'bi:n] **U5,** 85
Riverford Farm [rɪvəfɔ:d 'fɑ:m] **U6,** 93
Robbie Williams [rɒbi 'wɪljəmz] **U1,** 16
Royal Observatory [rɔɪəl əb'zɜ:vətri] **U4,** 60
⟨Sherlock Holmes⟩ [ʃɜ:lɒk 'həʊmz] **U6,** 105
Thomas Tallis School [tɒməs tælɪs 'sku:l] **U1,** 12
Will Young [wɪl 'jʌŋ] **U5,** 80
Wimbledon ['wɪmbldn] **U7,** 115
With Time [wɪð 'taɪm] **U5,** 80
Woodlands ['wʊdləndz] **U6,** 93
World Time ['wɜ:ld taɪm] **U4,** 65
X-Boys ['eks bɔɪz] **U5,** 81
XTM [eks ti: 'em] **U5,** 78
Venus Williams [vi:nəs 'wɪljəmz] **U7,** 115

A

abbiegen turn
Abend evening
abends in the evening
am Abend in the evening
den ganzen Abend lang all evening
zu Abend essen have dinner
Abendessen dinner
aber but
abholen fetch
Acker field
Aktivität activity
alle all
alleine alone
alles all
Alphabet alphabet
also so
alt old
Wie alt bist du? How old are you?
am on
am Abend in the evening
am Morgen in the morning
am Sonntag on Sunday
am Wochenende at the weekend
an at, to
anderer/andere/anderes other
anders different
anfangen start
anhaben wear
anhören listen, listen to
anrufen call, phone
Anrufer/Anruferin caller
anschauen watch, look at
ansehen look at
Antwort answer
antworten answer
Apfel apple
April April
Arbeit job, work
arbeiten work
Arbeitsblatt worksheet
Ärger trouble
auch also, too
auf at, on
auf Englisch in English
Auf Wiedersehen. Goodbye.
aufstehen get up
August August
aus from
ausfahren go out
ausgehen go out
ausprobieren try
außen outside
außerhalb outside
Austausch exchange
Auto car

B

Badezimmer bathroom
bald soon
Ball ball
Band band
Basketball basketball
Bauernhof farm
Baum tree
beantworten answer
bedeuten mean
beenden finish
bei with, at
bekommen get
belastet stressed
Belastung stress
belegtes Brot sandwich
bellen bark
beobachten watch
Beruf job
berühmt famous
beschäftigt busy
besitzen have got
besonderer, besondere, besonderes special
besorgt sein be worried
Besuch visit
besuchen visit
Bett bed
ins Bett gehen go to bed
beunruhigt sein be worried
bewölkt cloudy
Bibliothek library
Bild picture
bist are
bitte please
Bitte. You're welcome.
blau blue
Bleistift pencil
Boot boat
Boy Group boy band
braun brown
Brille glasses
Bruder brother
Buch book
Bücherei library
Buchstabe letter
Bude stall
Bulle bull
Bus bus
mit (dem Bus) by (bus)
Busch bush
Butter butter

C

Café café
Cafeteria cafeteria
Camcorder video camera
Cartoon cartoon
CD CD
Clown clown
Comicheft comic
Computer computer
cool cool
Cornflakes cornflakes
Cousin/Cousine cousin

D

da there
da drin in there
da ist there is
da sind there are
Dachboden attic
daheim at home
Damit basta! That's that!
danke (schön) thank you
Danke, gut. Fine, thanks.
dann then
das the, that
das ist this is
dasselbe the same
dein/deine your
denken think
der the
derselbe the same
deshalb this is why
Deutsch German
Deutschland Germany
Dezember December
dich you
dick big
die the
Dienstag Tuesday
diese these
dieselbe the same
dieser/diese/dieses this
dies ist this is
Ding thing
dir you
Diskjockey DJ
Disko disco
Diskus discus
diskutieren argue
Donnerstag Thursday
dort there
dort drin in there
draußen outside
du you
durstig thirsty
DVD DVD
DVD-Spieler DVD player

E

Ei egg
eigener, eigene, eigenes own
Einbruch break-in
ein/eine a, an
einfach easy

einige some
Eintrittskarte ticket
Eis ice cream
Eiscreme ice cream
Eltern parents
E-Mail e-mail
Ende end
England England
Engländer/Engländerin English
Ente duck
entlang along
Entschuldigung. Excuse me.
Entwurf design
er he
Ereignis event
erfinden make up
Ergebnis result
erzählen tell
es it
es gibt there is/there are
es ist there is
Es kostet .... It's ....
es sind there are
essen eat
Essen food, meal
Esszimmer dining room
etwas some
euch you
euer/eure your

F

fahren drive, go
mit ... fahren take
Fahrer/Fahrerin driver
Fahrrad bike
falsch wrong
Familie family
Fan fan
fantastisch fantastic
Welche Farbe hat ...? What colour is ...?
faul lazy
Februar February
Federmäppchen pencil case
Feld field
Fenster window
Ferien holiday
Fernseher television, TV
fertig ready
Festzug procession
Feuerwehrauto fire engine
Film film
Filzstift felt-tip
finden find
Fisch fish pl. fish
Fluss river
folgen follow
folglich so
Foto photo
Fotografie photo
Frage question
fragen ask
Frau woman pl. women, Mrs *(Anrede)*
Freitag Friday
Freizeitzentrum activity centre
fressen eat
Freund/Freundin boyfriend, friend
frisch fresh
froh happy
Frosch frog
Frühling spring
Frühstück breakfast
frühstücken have breakfast
Füller pen
funktionieren work
für for
furchtbar awful
Fußball football
füttern feed

G

Galaxie galaxy
Garten garden
Gaststätte restaurant
geben give
Geburtstag birthday
Herzlichen Glückwunsch zum Geburtstag! Happy birthday!
Gebüsch bush
gefährlich dangerous
gegenüber (von) opposite
gehen go, walk
Was geht hier vor? What's happening?
Wie geht's? How are you?
gelb yellow
Geld money
Gemüse vegetable
geöffnet open
geradeaus straight on
Geräusch noise
Gern geschehen. You're welcome.
gern haben like
gern mögen love
Geschäft shop
Geschenk present
Gesicht face
gestresst stressed
Getränk drink
Gewinn prize
gewinnen win
gewöhnlich usually
Gitarre guitar
Glas glass
Glück haben be lucky
glücklich happy
Golf golf
groß big, large
großartig great
grün green
Gruppe band, group
gut good
Guten Morgen. Good morning.
gut in good at

H

haben have got
halb half past
Hallo. Hello. / Hi.
Handy mobile phone
hart hard
hassen hate
Haus house
nach Hause home
Hausaufgaben homework
Hausmeister/Hausmeisterin caretaker
Haustier pet
Heft book
Heim home
heiß hot
heißen mean
Ich heiße .... My name is ....
Wie heißt du? What's your name?
heiter sunny
helfen help
Henne hen
herausfinden find out
Herbst autumn
Herr Mr *(Anrede)*
heute today
hier here
Hier bitte. Here you are.
hinein into
hinter behind
Hobby hobby
Hockey hockey
hoffen hope
holen fetch
hören hear, listen to
Hose trousers
Hotel hotel
Huhn hen
Hund dog
hundemüde dog-tired
Hut hat

I

ich I
ich besitze I've got
Ich bin .... I'm ....
ich habe I've got

Ich heiße .... My name is ....
Ich komme aus .... I'm from ....
Ich möchte .... I'd like to ....
Ich würde gerne .... I'd like to ....
Idee idea
ihm him
ihn him
ihnen them
ihr you
ihr/ihre her, their
Ihr/Ihre your
im in
Imbiss snack
immer always
in at, in, into
in der Nähe von near
in der Sendung on the programme
in der Stadt in town
ins Bett gehen go to bed
Indien India
Information information
Informationszentrum Information Centre
Inliner in-line skates
Inline-Skates in-line skates
in Ordnung fine, OK
interessant interesting
ist is
... ist hinter dir her ... is after you

J

ja yes
Jahr year
Jahrmarkt fair
Januar January
jeder everybody
jeder/jede/jedes every
jene those
jener/jene/jenes that
jetzt now
joggen gehen go jogging
Journalist/Journalistin journalist
Juli July
jung young
Junge boy
Juni June

K

Kaffee coffee
Kaffee trinken have a coffee
kalt cold
kämpfen fight
Kaninchen rabbit
kaputt broken
Karaoke karaoke
Kartentrick card trick
Käse cheese
Katze cat
kaufen buy
kennen know
kennen lernen meet
Schön dich kennen zu lernen. Nice to meet you.
Kinder children
Kinderschminken face painting
Kino cinema
Kirche church
Kiste box
Klasse *(in einer englischen Schule)* tutor group
Klasse sieben Year 7
Klassenzimmer classroom
Kleider clothes
Kleidung clothes
klein small
Kleintransporter van
klettern climb
klug clever
komisch funny
kommen come
Ich komme aus .... I'm from ....
Woher kommst du? Where are you from?
können can
Es **kostet ....** It's ....
Sie **kosten ....** They're ....
Wie viel **kosten** sie? How much are they?
Wie viel **kostet** es? How much is it?
Krankenpfleger nurse
Krankenschwester nurse
Kricket cricket
kriegen get
Küche kitchen
Küchenschrank cupboard
Kuchen cake
Kuh cow
Kunst art

L

Laden shop
Landkarte map
landwirtschaftliche Maschine farm machine
lang long
langweilig boring
Lärm noise
lass/lasst uns let's
Lass mich in Ruhe. Leave me alone.
Laterne lantern
laufen run, walk
leben live
legen put
Lego lego
Lehrer/Lehrerin teacher
leicht easy
Tut mir **Leid.** I'm sorry.
leise quiet
lesen read
Leute people
lieben love
Lieber/Liebe/Liebes *(in Briefanrede)* Dear
Lieblings- favourite
Lied song
Lieferwagen van
Lineal ruler
links left, on the left
Luftballon balloon
lustig funny

M

machen do, make
macht/machen Spaß is/are fun
Mädchen girl
Mahlzeit meal
Mai May
Mama mum
manchmal sometimes
Mann man pl. men
Mannschaft team
Markt market
März March
Maus mouse
Meerschweinchen guinea pig
meinen think
mein/meine my
Menschen people
Messer knife pl. knives
mich me
Milch milk
mir me
mit with
mit ... zusammen with
mit (dem Bus) by (bus)
mitnehmen take
zu **Mittag essen** have lunch
Mittagessen lunch
Mittagspause lunch break
Mittwoch Wednesday
Mobiltelefon mobile phone
Möchtest du ... ?/ Möchten Sie ... ? Would you like ...?
modern modern
mögen like, want to
Monat month
Monster monster

Montag Monday
morgen tomorrow
Morgen morning
am Morgen in the morning
Guten Morgen Good morning
morgens in the morning
müde tired
Musik music
müssen must
Muster design
Mutter mother

N

nach after, past, to
nach Hause home
nahe near
in der Nähe von near
Nahrung food
Name name
neben next to
nehmen take
nein no
nett nice
neu new
nicht not
nicht können can't
nicht mögen hate
nie never
niemals never
noch still
Norden north
normalerweise usually
November November
Nummer number
nun now
nur only

O

oder or
offen open
öffnen open
oft often
Oh. Oh.
OK OK
Oktober October
Oma grandma
Orangensaft orange juice
ordentlich tidy
Osten east

P

Paar pair
Papa dad
Park park
Parkplatz car park
Partner/Partnerin partner
Party party
eine Party feiern have a party
Pfad path
Pfund *(britische Währungseinheit)* pound
pink pink
Plan plan
Plappermaul chatterbox
Polizei police pl. police
Polizist/Polizistin police officer
Pony pony
Popstar pop star
Postamt post office
Poster poster
Preis prize
prima cool
Problem problem
Projekt project
Projekttag project day
Puzzle jigsaw puzzle

Q

Quiz quiz

R

Radiergummi rubber
Radio radio
Raum room
rechts right, on the right
reden mit talk to
reden über talk about
Regel rule
regnerisch rainy
rennen run
Rennen race
reparieren repair
Reporter/Reporterin reporter
Restaurant restaurant
Resultat result
richtig right
riesig large
Roboter robot
Rock skirt
rosa pink
rot red
Rucksack rucksack
rufen call
ruhig quiet

S

Sache thing
sagen say, tell
Samstag Saturday
Sandwich sandwich
sauber tidy
Schachtel box
Schaf sheep pl. sheep
schauen look
schenken give
scheußlich awful
schicken send
Schiff boat
schlafen sleep
schlafen gehen go to bed
Schlafsack sleeping bag
Schlafzimmer bedroom
Schlagzeug drums
schließen close
Schluss end
schmerzlich sad
schnell schmerzlich
Schokolade chocolate
schön nice
Schön dich kennen zu lernen. Nice to meet you.
Schrank cupboard
schreiben write
Schuh shoe
Schule school
Schüler/Schülerin pupil
Schulfest fair
Schulmannschaft school team
Schuppen shed
Schwamm sponge
Schwein pig
Schwester sister
schwierig hard
Schwierigkeiten trouble
Schwimmbad swimming pool
Schwimmbecken swimming pool
schwimmen gehen go swimming
sehen look
sehen see
Wir sehen uns dort. See you there.
sehr very
seid are
sein be
Sei/Seid leise. Be quiet.
sein/seine his
Semester term
senden send
Sendung programme
in der Sendung on the programme
September September
setzen put
sich ausdenken make up
sich prügeln fight
sich treffen meet
sich verlaufen get lost
sicher sure
sie she, her, them, they
Sie kosten .... They're ....
sind are

singen sing
sitzen sit
Skateboard skateboard
Snack snack
so so
Sofa sofa
Sommer summer
sonnig sunny
Sonntag Sunday
am Sonntag on Sunday
sonntags on Sunday
Sonst noch etwas? Anything else?
Speicher attic
Spiel game, play
spielen *(eine Rolle)* act, play
Spieler/Spielerin player
Spinne spider
Sport sports
Sportplatz sports field
Sport(arten) treiben do sports
sprechen speak
sprechen mit talk to
sprechen über talk about
Stadt town
in der Stadt in town
Stadtplan map
Stand stall
Star star
stehen stand
stellen put
Stern star
Stier bull
Strand beach
Straße road, street
streiten argue
Stress stress
Strichmännchen matchstick man pl. matchstick people
Stuhl chair
suchen look for
Süden south
Südwest- southwest
südwestlich southwest
Sweatshirt sweatshirt

T

Tafel board
Tag day
tanzen dance
Tasche bag
Taschenlampe torch
Tätigkeit activity
Taxi taxi
Team team
Tee tea
Teich pond
Teil part
teilnehmen an take part in
Telefon telephone
Tennis tennis
teuer expensive
Text text
Theaterstück play
Ticket ticket
Tier animal
Tisch table
Toast(brot) toast
Toilette toilet
toll fantastic
Tourist/Touristin tourist
tragen carry, wear *(von Kleidung)*
trainieren train
Traktor tractor
traurig sad
treffen meet
Treffpunkt meeting place
Trick trick
Trimester term
trinken drink
T-Shirt T-shirt
tun do, make
Tunnel tunnel
Tür door
Turnhalle sports hall
Turnier competition
Tut mir Leid. I'm sorry.

U

U-Bahn Underground
üben practise
über about, over
übernachten stay
Übungsheft exercise book
Uhr clock
... Uhr ... o'clock
Wie viel Uhr ist es? What time is it?
um at
um zu to
Umfrage survey
Umzug procession
und and
Ungeheuer monster
Uniform uniform
uns us
unser/unsere our
unter under
Unterführung tunnel
unterrichten teach
Urlaub holiday

V

Vater father
Veranstaltung event
Verbrecher/Verbrecherin criminal
... verfolgt dich ... is after you
verkaufen sell
verlassen leave
verregnet rainy
verrückt crazy
verschieden different
versuchen try
Vetter cousin
Videokamera video camera
viel much
viele lots of
vielleicht maybe
viertel nach quarter past
Vogel bird
Volleyball volleyball
von by, from
vor to, in front of
Vormittag morning
vorsichtig careful

W

wann when
warten wait
warum why
was what
Was geht hier vor? What's happening?
Was ist los? What's wrong?
waschen wash
Wasser water
weg away
Weg path
weglaufen vor run from
weil because
weitergehen go on
weitermachen go on
Weitsprung long jump
Welche Farbe hat ...? What colour is ...?
welcher/welche/welches which, what
Weltzeit *(erste Zeitzone)*
wer who
werfen throw
Westen west
Wettbewerb competition
Wetter weather
Wettkampf competition
wie how
Wie alt bist du? How old are you?
Wie geht's? How are you?
Wie heißt du? What's your name?
Wie viel kosten sie? How much are they?
Wie viel kostet es? How much is it?
Wie viel Uhr ist es? What time is it?

wieder again
Auf **Wiedersehen.** Goodbye.
wild wild
Winter winter
wir us, we
wirklich really
Wir sehen uns dort. See you there.
wissen know
Witz joke
wo where
Woche week
Wochenende weekend
am Wochenende at the weekend
Woher kommst du ? Where are you from ?
wohin where
wohnen live, stay
Wohnung flat
Wohnzimmer living room
wolkig cloudy
wollen want to
Wort word
wütend angry

Z

Zeichentrickfilm cartoon
zeichnen draw
zeigen show
Zeit time
die Zeiten messen take the times
Zelt tent
Zimmer room
zornig angry
zu too, to
Zug train
zu Hause at home
Zuhause home
zuhören listen
zurück back
zusehen watch

Grammar words

Dies sind die wichtigsten englischen Grammatikwörter in Let's go. *Du hast sie auf den „Grammar"-Seiten kennen gelernt. Sie helfen dir, über die englische Sprache zu sprechen.*

Present simple *(einfache Gegenwart)*	I often **listen** to the radio.
Present progressive *(Verlaufsform)*	She'**s listening** to the radio now.
Singular *(Einzahl)*	one book
Plural *(Mehrzahl)*	two books
Genitive *(besitzanzeigendes s)*	This is Tom'**s** rucksack.
Apostrophe *(Apostroph)*	Tom's
Possessive pronouns *(besitzanzeigendes Fürwort)*	**my** book, **his** computer, **her** ball
Imperative *(Befehlsform)*	**Open** the door!
Negative imperative *(verneinte Befehlsform)*	**Don't do** crazy things!

Numbers

1 = one	10 = ten	20 = twenty	30 = thirty
2 = two	11 = eleven	21 = twenty-one	40 = forty
3 = three	12 = twelve	22 = twenty-two	50 = fifty
4 = four	13 = thirteen	23 = twenty-three	60 = sixty
5 = five	14 = fourteen	24 = twenty-four	70 = seventy
6 = six	15 = fifteen	25 = twenty-five	80 = eighty
7 = seven	16 = sixteen	26 = twenty-six	90 = ninety
8 = eight	17 = seventeen	27 = twenty-seven	100 = one hundred
9 = nine	18 = eighteen	28 = twenty-eight	
	19 = nineteen	29 = twenty-nine	

In the classroom

Dies ist eine Liste der wichtigsten Arbeitsanweisungen in Let's go. *Deine Lehrerin oder dein Lehrer benutzt sie, wenn du etwas tun sollst:*

Act the dialogue with a partner.	*Spiele das Gespräch mit einem Partner nach.*
And you?	*Und du?*
Answer the questions.	*Beantworte die Fragen.*
Ask a friend / a partner.	*Frage einen Freund/einen Partner.*
Can you find the numbers?	*Kannst du die Nummern finden?*
Come to the board, please.	*Komm bitte an die Tafel.*
Go on, please.	*Mach bitte weiter.*
Is that right?	*Ist das richtig?*
Listen and speak.	*Höre zu und sprich nach.*
Look at the pictures.	*Schau dir die Bilder an.*
Listen to the dialogues.	*Höre dir die Dialoge an.*
Make a poster with pictures and words.	*Mache ein Poster mit Bildern und Wörtern.*
Make a word web in your exercise book.	*Mache ein Wortnetz in deinem Übungsheft.*
Make picture words with the words.	*Mache Wortbilder mit den Wörtern.*
Make dialogues with a partner.	*Mache Dialoge mit einem Partner.*
Make pairs.	*Bildet Paare.*
Make sentences / questions.	*Bilde Sätze/Fragen.*
Make two groups.	*Bildet zwei Gruppen.*
Match the names with the dates.	*Ordne die Namen den Daten zu.*
Match the parts of the sentences.	*Ordne die Satzteile einander zu.*
Now act the dialogue.	*Nun spiele das Gespräch nach.*
Open your books at page 15.	*Schlagt eure Bücher auf Seite 15 auf.*
Right or wrong?	*Richtig oder falsch?*
Say it in English.	*Sag es auf Englisch.*
Talk about your hobbies.	*Sprich über deine Hobbies.*
What can you see in the picture?	*Was siehst du auf dem Bild?*
What colour is it?	*Welche Farbe hat er/sie/es?*
What's in the rucksack?	*Was ist in dem Rucksack?*
What's missing?	*Was fehlt?*
Who is it?	*Wer ist es?*
What's the right order?	*Was ist die richtige Reihenfolge?*
What's the right word?	*Was ist das richtige Wort?*
Write questions.	*Schreibe Fragen auf.*

Das kannst du sagen, wenn du etwas tun möchtest oder ein Problem hast:

Can I go outside, please?	*Darf ich bitte hinausgehen?*
Can I go to the toilet, please?	*Kann ich bitte auf die Toilette gehen?*
Can I open the window, please?	*Kann ich bitte das Fenster aufmachen?*
Can I work with …?	*Kann ich mit … zusammenarbeiten?*
Can we sing a song/play a game?	*Können wir ein Lied singen/ein Spiel machen?*
Can you help me, please?	*Können Sie/Kannst du mir bitte helfen?*
I don't understand this.	*Ich verstehe das hier nicht.*
Pardon?	*Wie bitte?*
Sorry, I haven't got my homework.	*Entschuldigung, ich habe meine Hausaufgaben nicht.*
What's that in German?	*Wie heißt das auf Deutsch?*

Quellen

Bildquellen: Umschlag: Ernst Klett Verlag/Fletcher; Vorderer Vorsatz: Mauritius Images (O'Brien) Stuttgart, (Cutty Sark); Ernst Klett Verlag/Fletcher (Kinder); S. 8: Ernst Klett Verlag/Fletcher; S. 9: Ernst Klett Verlag/Fletcher; S. 10: Ernst Klett Verlag/Fletcher; S. 11: Photodisc; S. 12: Ernst Klett Verlag/Fletcher; S. 13: Ernst Klett Verlag/Fletcher; S. 14: Ernst Klett Verlag/Smith; S. 17: Ernst Klett Verlag/Fletcher; S. 28: Corbis (Nik Wheeler), Düsseldorf (Häuser): Ernst Klett Verlag/Fletcher (Familien); S. 29: Corbis (Tom Bearn), Düsseldorf (Gebäude): Ernst Klett Verlag/Fletcher (Familien); S. 32: Ernst Klett Verlag/Fletcher; S. 44: Ernst Klett Verlag/Fletcher; S. 45: Ernst Klett Verlag/Fletcher; S. 46: mecom (ddp/Gerhard Blank), Hamburg (DJ): Getty Images (Photodisc), München (Junge); S. 48: Corbis (Larry Williams), Düsseldorf (Mädchen): mecom (ddp/Gerhard Blank), Hamburg (DJ); S. 50: Corbis (Dale C. Spartas); S. 60: Corbis (Eye Ubiquitous/Julia Waterlow), Düsseldorf (Greenwich): National Maritime Museum, London (Meridian Line): Topham Picturepoint (UPPA Ltd), Edenbridge Kent (Cutty Sark); S. 61: Collections Picture Gallery (HAG-12846-1), London (Greenwich Market); S. 62: © Maps in a Minute; S. 63: Ernst Klett Verlag/Fletcher; S. 64: Ernst Klett Verlag/Fletcher; S. 68: Mel Smith Photography, Nottingham (Tourist Information): © Corel Corporation, Unterschleissheim (Kirche, Schwimmbad, Café): Corbis (Firefly Productions), Düsseldorf (Parkanlage); S. 69: © Corel Corporation, Unterschleissheim (Restaurant); S. 71: Punch Library (Donega), London (cartoon); S. 73: Mirror Syndication International, London; S. 77: Ernst Klett Verlag/Fletcher; S. 78: Ernst Klett Verlag/Fletcher; S. 80: Ernst Klett Verlag/Fletcher; S. 81: Ernst Klett Verlag/Fletcher (Lisa); Corbis (James Leynse); S. 83: Getty Images (Foodpix/Susan C. Bourgoin), München; S. 92: Corbis (Robert Gill, Papilio), Düsseldorf (Strand); Devon Guide Touristique, unbekannter Lieferant (Karte); S. 93: Unbekannter Lieferant (Woodlands Leisure Park): Dartmoorsafaris, Stoke, Plymouth, Devon (Safaris): Soil Association (Rupert Aker), Bristol (Riverford Farm): Unbekannter Lieferant (Devon Farms); S. 100: The Cartoon Book, Dobbs Ferry, NY (cartoons); Corbis, Düsseldorf (Mädchen, Junge); S. 101: Europa-Park, Rust; S. 106: Das Fotoarchiv (Markus Dlouhy), Essen (Disco): Fotosearch RF (Photodisc), Waukesha, WI 53186-1898 (Laternen): Corbis (Robbie Jack), Düsseldorf (Bugsy Malone); S. 107: Topham Picturepoint, Edenbridge Kent (Sport, Schulfest); S. 109: MEV, Augsburg; S. 115: Ernst Klett Verlag/Fletcher (schwarzes Brett): Das Fotoarchiv (Rupert Oberhaeuser), Essen (Disco); S. 117: From: The Music Makers, © Christian Verlag, München 1979/Foto: Erich Auerbach; S. 119: Corbis (Galen Rowell), Düsseldorf; S. 120: Ernst Klett Verlag/Fletcher; S. 121: Ernst Klett Verlag/Fletcher; S. 122: Unbekannter Lieferant, Stuttgart

Textquellen: S. 11: © 1955 by Mark VII Ltd., für D/A/CH/GUS+osteur. Länder: Neue Welt Musikverlag, GmbH, München; S. 55: © 1995 Penguin Books Ltd; S. 89: Adapted from Mind-Bending Lateral Thinking Puzzles by Jenny Lynch © Lagoon Books; S. 117: T+M: John Lennon and Paul McCartney © Northern Songs. Used by permission of Music Sales Ltd. All rights reserved. International Copyright Control